"The power of *Secrets from a Prison* looks the reader directly in the eye, r or excuses for crime, and demonstr forgiveness are mutually enforcing, not in current failed system would have us believe. After reading this book, it will be all of us—citizens, leaders, teachers, clergy, law-makers—who are left naked and morally compromised if we fail to act to transform a soul-crushing system of retribution into a process and means of restoration. Tony Vick has given us the gift of discomfort. May we use it well."

—**Jeannie Alexander**, Director, No Exceptions Prison Collective

"Prisons reveal the secreted nature of the regime that creates them. Two millennia ago John of Patmos pulled back the veil and exposed Rome's monstrous essence. Seven decades ago, Elie Wiesel's revelations of the concentration camps unmasked the sadistic bloodlust of the Nazi's reign. In this tradition Tony Vick's exposé of the prison-industrial complex divulges the concealed character of the American Empire. Like John's and Elie's revelations, Tony's call is neither for despair nor pity. No, here is a summons to action. Read this book and you must join the Resistance."

—**Richard C. Goode**, Lipscomb University

"2.2 million people are in US prisons and jails, with millions more on probation and parole, but such statistics about our ever-expanding carceral society tend to prove powerless at touching hearts or even minds. Tony Vick's stories and poems have the creative power of word and image to make the prisoner's life task of correction and rehabilitation a contribution to the urgently needed conversation among and within ourselves about who we are and what we might become as twenty-first–century Americans."

—**Bruce T. Morrill**, Professor, Vanderbilt Divinity School

Secrets from a Prison Cell

Secrets from a Prison Cell

*A Convict's Eyewitness Account of the Dehumanizing
Drama of Life Behind Bars*

Tony D. Vick

WITH
Michael T. McRay

FOREWORD BY
Richard Rohr

CASCADE *Books* · Eugene, Oregon

SECRETS FROM A PRISON CELL
A Convict's Eyewitness Account of the Dehumanizing Drama of Life
Behind Bars

Cascade Books
An Imprint of Wipf and Stock Publishers
199 W. 8th Ave., Suite 3
Eugene, OR 97401

www.wipfandstock.com

PAPERBACK ISBN: 978-1-4982-9433-1
HARDCOVER ISBN: 978-1-4982-9435-5
EBOOK ISBN: 978-1-4982-9434-8

Cataloguing-in-Publication data:

Names: Vick, Tony D. | McRay, Michael T. | Rohr, Richard, foreword.

Title: Secrets from a prison cell : a convict's eyewitness account of the
dehumanizing drama of life behind bars / Tony D. Vick with Michael T.
McRay.

Description: Eugene, OR: Cascade Books, 2018 | Includes bibliographical references.

Identifiers: ISBN 978-1-4982-9433-1 (paperback) | ISBN 978-1-4982-
9435-5 (hardcover) | ISBN 978-1-4982-9434-8 (ebook)

Subjects: LCSH: Prisons. | Prisoners. | United States. | Poetry. | LBGTQ.
| Title.

Classification: HV9871 .V53 2018 (print) | HV9871 .V53 (ebook)

Manufactured in the U.S.A.   01/26/18

To Cindy Ford

There is a really deep pit. I live there, and God dwells there with me. On occasion, it is quite difficult for me to find him within the darkness of my soul. At those moments, he sends a beloved creation to communicate in terms I can understand, a creation whose voice I can hear, whose hands I can feel, and whose eyes I can see—to sit with me and remind me to just hang on.

Cindy, my debt to you can never be repaid.

There are a few seconds each morning where I find myself in complete peace. The moments, just as I am waking up—before I succumb to the realization of my existence. It's the time of the day before the look, the feel, the taste of prison envelops me. In these moments, I am free, and equal to all humanity.

Contents

Foreword—Fr. Richard Rohr, OFM | ix

Preface—Michael T. McRay | xiii

Acknowledgments | xix

    When You Smell a Flower | xxi

1   I Am Prisoner #276187 | 1

    I Was, I Am | 5

2   I'm Hungry, Feed Me | 6

    Break Bread With Me | 12

3   Cutting Through the Pain | 13

    My Cocoon | 17

    Stay With Me | 19

4   Beyond the Living Room | 20

    I See a Home | 24

5   The Art of Redemption | 25

    The Perfect House | 30

6   A Little Kindness | 31

    Endless Love | 33

CONTENTS

7   Sentenced To Death: By Old Age | 34

    I Shall Not Die Alone | 40

    Maybe Tonight | 41

8   Monsters Don't Live Under the Bed | 42

    In Those Moments | 48

    Taking Flight | 49

9   Buster | 50

    My hands touched God's hands today | 58

    Once a Slave . . . Always a Slave? | 59

10 Is It Just This? | 61

    Is It Just This? | 64

    it's not what i imagined | 65

11 Wheelchairs, Walkers, and Wishes | 66

    Walk On | 70

12 Say No to Photoshopping | 71

    Reality Monster | 75

13 Hanging On in Tandem | 77

    Hang On | 80

14 It Is Possible | 83

    Change: It Is Possible | 93

    It's Been Too Long | 94

    About the Authors:

    Tony D. Vick | 95

    Michael T. McRay | 97

    Bibliography | 99

Foreword

Even though both John the Baptist and St. Paul spent much time imprisoned, as did Saints Francis of Assisi, Ignatius of Loyola, John of the Cross, and many others throughout Christian history, it is amazing to me that there is so little awareness of the needs, hopes, and possibilities of the incarcerated in most Christian communities. They are still "other" people who are "over there" and largely invisible to our daily lives and interests. Yet jails and prisons have often served as would-be monasteries, seminaries, hermitages, altar calls, and retreat houses—hotbeds of human transformation.

Even in the classic listing of the six "corporal works of mercy" that were expected of all believers going back to the first millennium of Christianity, one of the six is listed as "visiting the imprisoned" and in some listings, it was put more bravely as "ransoming the captives"! At least one religious order took an actual vow to do just that!

A man called St. Peter Nolasco in 1218 Spain required of himself and his followers a special vow to devote their "whole substance and very liberty to the ransoming of slaves and the wrongly imprisoned," even to the point of acting as hostages for them. According to records, the "Order of our Lady of Ransom" accomplished approximately 70,000 rescues—some 2,700 during Peter's own lifetime.

They still exist, although in small numbers, and are commonly called "Mercedarians" because of their complete commitment to showing mercy (*merced* in Spanish) to the powerless, the enslaved, and the falsely imprisoned. Many of them later accompanied the conquistadors to the New World to do the same, first for the indigenous peoples and later the slaves. What a shame that they were not the dominant form of Christianity, and today few even know about this too easily forgotten history. Perhaps their existence was a judgment on the rest of us?

Mostly, I fear it reveals the highly establishment position in which most Christian denominations and individuals found themselves after we ourselves moved from the Roman catacombs to the palaces, after the Emperor Constantine made us the official religion of the Empire, starting in 313 AD. We were no longer the persecuted, but too often ourselves became the persecutors. We radically changed sides and perspectives.

Now why do I mention this in the foreword to Tony Vick's fine book? I do it to make us aware of how much our Christian perspective has changed over the centuries. In most cases, we no longer look *up* at society from the servant position of Jesus, but instead began to look *down* at prisoners, the incarcerated, and the powerless in general—from our now established and comfortable position. Anyone in jail now is usually assumed to be likely wrong, bad, or at least deserving of just punishment. This despite the now weekly DNA tests that prove how many people have been judged and imprisoned unjustly and falsely still in the modern "scientific" and just law period. Our bias is firmly in place, I am afraid.

I myself was a prison chaplain here in Albuquerque, New Mexico for fourteen years, and got to learn from many thousands of incarcerated people during that time. It was amazing to me how many of them eventually came to see their time in jail almost as a monastery, but now with all the historic vows of "poverty, chastity, and obedience" imposed on them by necessity. But many used it to very good soul advantage—their own and others.

Many developed a very real prayer life, a commitment to spiritual reading and Bible study, and a true love of God and service of neighbor during both short and more extended sentences. I cannot say it was the norm, but it was amazingly common. There are lots of little saints hidden away in jails! Many prisoners have

used their just or unjust punishment to become highly transformed people, just like John the Baptist, Paul, Francis, Ignatius,
and John of the Cross.

You are now privileged to meet such a man, who has hum-
bly written to me for many years, and some of his stories that will
beautifully exemplify the truth of what I just said. Maybe he can
help to change your—and the culture's—perspective from the top
down to the bottom up, and from the familiar center to the too
unfamiliar edge, where the saints and prophets so often live.

Fr. Richard Rohr, OFM

Center for Action and Contemplation
Albuquerque, New Mexico
December 2016

Preface

I walked out into the August sun to get the mail at the end of my gravel driveway. I didn't expect to find much of interest, as most days the mailbox seemed stuffed with United Airlines promotions or a reminder that a better credit card deal is always one application away. But pulling down the rubber lid, I found a manila envelope addressed to me in familiar handwriting. It was from Tony Vick.

A month earlier, I had sent a card and picture to my dear friend, held captive in a Tennessee prison hours from my Nashville home, to tell him my good news: "She said yes! On Saturday, July 2, I asked Brittany to marry me and she agreed. It happened—I'm engaged!" A few weeks later, he had called while I was with Brittany, and she smiled to hear at last his quick Southern drawl come through the phone: "So sorry I won't be able to make it to your wedding," he said. "I wish I could." Then he paused before his joke. "But if you see helicopters overhead during the ceremony, you'll know I'm coming. But don't worry—I'll just stay long enough for cake!" I cannot remember a single conversation with Tony where I didn't laugh. When we hung up, Brittany said, "I didn't realize it until that conversation, but that's how I've always imagined the voice of God." I thought of God's sound belonging to a gay incarcerated poet, and I was happy.

When I opened the package from Tony, I found something unexpected. Though he could not attend our ceremony or offer anything from the registry, he still sent a gift. He had glued two pieces of cardboard together and covered them in ornate, cutout decorations of flowers, rabbits, wedding images, and more. On computer paper, he had printed, "She said yes!" and pasted it in different colors all over the makeshift canvas. On the back were quotations and poems on love and marriage—some quirky, others sentimental. On the front, amidst even more quotations and images, were two rectangles cut out of the cardboard revealing the picture I'd sent him of Brittany and me the evening of our engagement, as well as the portion of the card quoted above telling him she said yes. Brittany and I have Tony's gift displayed proudly in our home library, a reminder of the inability of prison walls to separate love and friendship.

I tell you this story so that you might have some idea of the kind of man Tony is.

I first met Tony in 2011 on a Saturday night at Riverbend Maximum Security Institution in Nashville. Nearly every Saturday for several years, we both sat around a table together—alongside other prison insiders and Free World volunteers—as part of a contemplative prayer group. I had gotten involved at the invitation of my friend and former professor Richard Goode and felt my Christian faith compelled me to journey behind prison walls. Each Saturday, amid discussions regarding whatever text we'd read that week, Tony always showed up with a comment or question of piercing insight or one so hilarious we struggled not to fall from our chairs. Tony helped us all remember that even in times of prayer and worship, laughter can be as holy as reverence.

When meeting Tony, though one is often struck first by his quick wit and beautiful Southern drawl, you'll soon see his true character: tender, generous, hospitable, and magnificent in love. It does not take long to see the real Tony because some time ago, he stopped hiding behind masks and false stories about himself. As you'll learn in his first chapter, Tony is incarcerated because of two murders stemming from a lie he told himself about himself, a violent narrative his church and community fed him about the source of his worth. To be saved, Tony heard from pastors and peers, one must at least be straight. Tony knew he wasn't straight and feared he might not be saved, and so he suppressed who he was to pretend he was who everyone else wanted him to be. Strangely enough, Tony's story reminds me of fantasy film.

A few weeks ago, Brittany and I went to see *Fantastic Beasts and the Where to Find Them*, a new movie set in the world of Harry Potter. In the film, a destructive dark cloud called an *obscurus* wreaks havoc on the city. The *obscurus*, we learn, is essentially a type of parasite that forms when a wizard suppresses magical abilities, denying to themselves and the world the true nature of their identity. This parasite expands into a violent spirit that manipulates and morphs the host into a wrecking ball that decimates all in its path. The *obscurus* can only find a home when one refuses to welcome one's true self, and thus the unwelcomed self becomes the agent for violence.

In this way, Tony had an *obscurus*. Told even at a young age that his interest in other boys was the stuff of damnation, Tony tried, quite tragically, to be a straight man. Soon, his *obscurus* struck and the aftermath left two women dead, a child traumatized and parentless, families heartbroken, and Tony in prison. Ironically, it was in the confinement of prison that Tony finally found his freedom. Realizing the consequences of life lived in denial, Tony began to greet each part of himself he'd till then rejected and found a welcome and shelter in himself he'd thirsted for his whole life. In some informal reflections he called "Coming In, Coming Out," Tony wrote of a moment of radical acceptance. Standing naked in his cell alone, he gazed across his bare body through a small handheld mirror—a body whose desires he'd denied for decades, a body his *obscurus* had turned into a weapon—and he spoke words of love over every inch of himself. Tears flowing, Tony at last recognized that who he was could be accepted, and he felt, perhaps for the first time, that who he was had been loved by God this whole time. That moment was Tony's baptism, not by water but by self-love. He died to his old self and was reborn into a life of authenticity.

Meeting Tony now, it seems impossible he's guilty of such horrible harms. His transformation is true, and his authenticity is inspiring. Each day, Tony decides to live—to really live—as full and as happy a life as possible, despite his incarceration. This is his resistance; this is how he fights the dehumanization of confinement. American prisons today are designed to suffocate the soul. They bruise, burden, and break the bodies and hopes of those exiled there, carving into their psyche a sense of disposability. "Abandon hope all ye who enter here." But Tony Vick has not consented to be caged. The Tennessee Department of Corrections (TDOC) holds his body captive, but it cannot crush his spirit. Despite the TDOC's best efforts, Tony continues to live as fully and joyfully as possible in the world he inhabits.

In this book, Tony brings this authenticity and freedom before you. He shortens the distance between the Free World and the invisible world of incarceration. For some time, Tony has recognized his responsibility to bear witness to the realities of prison life, and he pulled back the curtain in a series of essays that his dearly loved friend Cindy Ford emailed to a group of Free World folk. Toward the end of 2015, I suggested to Tony that we try publishing his essays as a book. While grateful for my confidence in him, he seemed less certain his writing was worthy of a contract. I remain thankful to the good people of Cascade Books for proving him wrong.

Secrets from a Prison Cell is a gift. In it, Tony brings us proximate to the sounds and sights of prison. Through the wit and wisdom present in each conversation Tony has, he tells us his secrets—in stories and poetry. For a few readers, the secrets may be of the true demonic nature of incarceration. These may be stories you've never heard before. Warehousing, shipping, shackles—perhaps you've not known that humans are still subjected to such slavery. But for me, these are not the secrets Tony means to tell us. That violence exists in prison is no secret. That people are raped and abused and dehumanized is no secret. The secret, which too few of us seemed to have heard before, is that those we've locked away are the very mirrors of our society, both the good and ill. In prison, there is art. In prison, there is community and friendship. In prison, there is generosity, love, compassion, and kindness. In prison, there is meaning to be found where meaning is scarce. In prison, there are answers to some of the questions most urgently in need of our attention.[1] In prison, there are caged birds singing freedom songs. And these secrets are worth telling. Why should such truths stay hidden?

Whatever your situation, I invite you to consider Tony Vick's words. We will never find the healing and reconciliation this world so desperately needs if we acquiesce to walls of fear, if we consent to narratives of disposability, if we accept that some of us are less valuable than others of us. For those who may never be able to set foot behind prison walls, *Secrets from a Prison Cell* gives you another way inside. May this book get us one step closer to a world where no one is cast aside, where the stories in this book are the stories we will tell to remind us of days long gone that we hope never to see again.

Turn the page now. The caged bird sings. Listen.

Michael T. McRay

Nashville, Tennessee
December 2016

---

1. Language in these last two lines inspired by Pádraig Ó Tuama's poem "The Facts of Life" in *Sorry for Your Troubles*, 7–8.

Acknowledgments

Seeing this book come to be has been a marvelous dream come true. My twenty years in prison have convinced me that it's very important for others to know what is happening to prison inmates. Are they receiving treatment, education, training, and therapy to combat and defeat the demons that brought them to prison, or are they victims of a mismanaged system that leaves them unprotected and vulnerable to emotional trauma, gang violence, drugs, and sexual abuse?

It may seem odd that I appreciate witnessing and hearing the many difficult life stories that comprise my essays and poetry, but strangely I do. So many inmates have experienced profound tragedies without ever letting anyone else know. As pain-filled as these stories are, hearing them was a privilege and being permitted to retell them in my book is an honor. I hope I have done them justice.

I am fortunate to have many friends who have left prison and now are living in Freedomsville. Each has given me special gifts in his own unique way: Randall, Larry, Ryan, Drac, T. W., Steve, and many others.

I am also grateful for the faithful pen pals who have lifted me and carried me through many dark moments while sharing their lives with me through pen and paper. Thank you, Sue, Lyn, Becky, Claudette, Gigi, Charmaine, Julie, and Sam.

During my time at Riverbend prison in Nashville, I was part of a contemplative prayer group for volunteers and inmates who gathered at the prison each Saturday night to study and pray together. Their words and love have changed my life. Many thanks to

Richard, Bruce, Matt, Dan, Andrew, Forrest, Valerie, Marie Claire, Dusty, Ben, Ed, and Jorge.

To my friends who remain in prison and are now scattered around the state, you are always a part of my heart: Jacob, Dean, Jamie, Woody, Chad, and Art.

I give special thanks to Jeannie Alexander, the former prison chaplain who taught me how to see God in the midst of such hate and chaos and who encouraged me to write about it.

Special thanks also to Michael McRay, my coauthor. Your generosity and dedication have been key in bringing this book to publication—you are amazing.

I am especially grateful for Cindy Ford and for her husband, John Ford—y'all are the smartest, most loving, hardworking hands of God I have seen on earth. This is as much your project as it is mine. Thank you for believing in me and all the men and women who are incarcerated and just trying to hang on.

I am deeply honored that Fr. Richard Rohr, a world-renowned scholar, author, and spiritual leader, has written the foreword for my book. Thank you, Fr. Richard. Your books, your support, and your love have deeply touched my heart for many years.

To my new friends at Cascade, especially Rodney Clapp and Calvin Jaffarian, thank you for believing in me and agreeing to publish my book.

Many thanks also go again to Richard Goode, Bruce Morrill, and Jeannie Alexander, who wrote such kind remarks about this book. I'm humbled by your words.

And to the thousands of incarcerated men and women: You are seen, you are heard, you are loved.

When You Smell a Flower ──────────────

When you smell a flower
    Do you pluck it from the ground
        and bring it to your nose?
    Are you in a green field dotted with
        spots of wild, vibrant colors?
    Are you receiving a bouquet of
        fragrant roses from a lover?
    Are you standing at a coffin where
        tribute blooms blanket the sleeping box?
        When you smell a flower

When you smell a flower
    you are amidst life, love,
    excitement, sadness.
        When you smell a flower

When I smell a flower
    It's a phantom of a memory needed to
    conjure up a feeling of good, hope, love,
    but it's a mirage in the field of stone.
        When I smell a flower

1

I Am Prisoner #276187

I am prisoner #276187, otherwise known as Tony Vick, a convicted double murderer, serving two well-deserved life sentences in the Tennessee Department of Correction. In 1993, I killed my first wife, the only girl I had ever dated, and in 1996, I killed my second wife, the only other woman I had ever dated. Both women were beautiful, wonderful, loving people who fell in love with the man I had created from lies and manipulations. You see, for thirty-four years of my life, I held a secret—I was gay.

Forty years ago, saying these words, "I am gay," was not as easy as it is today. Being a good Southern Baptist meant that being homosexual would send you straight to hell, and I believed in hell. Most Sundays from the pulpit, the preacher painted vivid pictures of such a place of eternal torment. The religious folk said that God could cure any disease, and, to them, homosexuality was a disease of the mind. However, with enough faith, one could be set free from such a miserable curse. I prayed and prayed, repented and repented, asking God to take the wicked thoughts out of my mind. When he didn't, I had to accept that I did not have enough faith to warrant such a miracle.

As a teenager, I finally sought the advice of a preacher. He told me that I needed to walk the walk and talk the talk of a heterosexual man, and that eventually my heart would catch up. He insisted that God was waiting for me to accept his miracle and live accordingly. So, I took a girl to my high school fall dance and eventually married her. Surely this would show God that I was serious about receiving his miracle.

The miracle didn't come, and, close to my thirtieth birthday, the thought of living another day with my lies didn't seem possible. Instead of telling the truth and facing the consequences, I chose a coward's way and an illogical path by killing my wife. I had created such a web of deceit that I didn't recognize myself. I felt lost, to God and to the world. God, I thought, could forgive anything, including murder, but could not tolerate or forgive homosexuality. Even though I had never acted out any of my fantasies of being with a man, the thoughts alone were forbidden sins that required God's healing hands. My entire life became one big lie, and everything I said and did was formed out of an alternate reality.

After my wife's death was ruled accidental, I thought surely this was a sign from God that he was trying to heal me. So, sometime later, I married my widowed neighbor, a friend, and was going to try again to walk the walk and talk the talk. I had to find the faith to be healed. I did not, and my marriage ended the same way—murder. Two women, their families, their friends, and their community were all devastated by my selfish, cowardly acts of lying, manipulating, and killing. There is no way to justify or rationalize my choices. They were all mine. I was convicted, and now I'm in prison where I deserve to be. Even this place, with all of its horrors, can't punish me enough for my sins. Nor can it add any more grief or remorse to my heart than my own mind already has. Am I crazy? I don't know. I'm just me, mixed up, confused, scared. The "why" of it all can't be explained, at least not by me. The thirty-four years I lived in the Free World are valleys of time that I wish could be erased. But that's not how life works; it is what it is, for better or for worse.

My first years in prison were spent barely existing, walking around like a zombie without any real emotion, trying not to feel anything—seemingly dead inside, unworthy of happiness, kindness, or life. I lacked the courage to kill myself. I had proven that by killing others instead. In that pit of despair is where I really found God, the same one who had been there all along. I had spent so much time trying to be what I heard man tell me to be that I failed to be quiet and listen—to be still. I didn't hear an audible voice from the Almighty, nor did I have a burning bush moment where life's secrets were revealed. What I did find was calmness, peace, and a slow realization that God loved me, just as I was. I found that his love and forgiveness were enough to cover all the evil I had done.

I believe God has forgiven me, but forgiving myself has been a more difficult process, one that perhaps will never be fully complete. The miracle of forgiveness seems so incredible that it's hard to simply accept. But if I didn't constantly remind myself that it's possible, I would wither away at the bottom of a pit. I don't expect forgiveness from my victims' families, friends, or communities. The scars I left are likely too deep to ever heal. Scars were also left on my own family, who became victims themselves. My parents and brother have died since my incarceration, but, while alive, they suffered greatly as a result of my sins. And my precious son, just a young child when I entered prison and now a grown man, has spent his childhood, teenage years, and now his adulthood burdened with the sins of his father. My choices robbed so many people of their hopes, dreams, and, perhaps, a countless number of great things my victims might have achieved. Unforgiveable by human hearts. I understand.

I can't cast blame on the church or the preachers for my crimes, nor can I blame my gayness. Many people have faced similar challenges and have not destroyed other lives in order to gain their own authenticity. All I have to blame are the dominoes of lies that I lined up beginning early in my life. I finally tipped one over, beginning a ripple effect of destruction. They fell hard and for a long time. All the dominoes have now stopped falling, but the tumbled masses of debris is left as a constant reminder of my deceit that created them and the forces that pushed that first domino over—all my actions.

But here I am, still alive, breathing, feeling, thinking. Unfair? Yes. Nonetheless, a reality. Prison forced me to drop my veil of deception. God gave his forgiveness, and now I'm left with the question, what to do? Prison is my community now, full of broken people and souls needing love and a voice. My hope is to share the experience of incarceration with a world that may be surprised at the true state of our prisons and the emotional trauma experienced inside the razor-wire fences.

Why is this important? Most inmates will get out of prison. Some will even be your neighbors. Some will be working for you or with you. Some will be serving you food at a restaurant. Some will be around your children. Some will be everywhere you go. So, it's important that, while your tax dollars are funding their stints behind bars, inmates receive treatment, education, and other preparation to live successfully without re-victimizing the community in the Free World. One thing is for sure: you cannot put a tiger in a cage, throw him a crumb occasionally, keep him from human contact and love, continually poke him with a stick, and think that, when the cage is opened, he will become a house kitty.

I hope you will receive these essays and poems from the flawed creature that I am. I have attempted to paint a picture of prison for you to experience and interpret. Then, you can decide for yourself if you can comfortably hang this picture on the wall of your world. Or is it too disturbing?

I Was, I Am

I was an emotional dictator
>tunnel visioned to see only my path
>my needs, wants, pain, fear

I was a liar and a manipulator
>truth simply a relative suggestion
>using words to form a new reality

I was a masked queer hiding from the truth
>dirty, an abomination, hell bound

I was a murderer
>breaths of life taken by me
>>by me   by me

I am a listener of life's stories
>quiet, reflective, open

I am a truth teller
>it is what it is
>not made up in a hopeful mind

I am gay and open to the world
>not formed by man's evil interpretation
>but created by God's hands

I am a sinner
>forgiven by God
>>by God   by God

I am prisoner #276187

2

I'm Hungry, Feed Me

Food is the ultimate equalizer. We cannot live without it, and most of us spend countless hours satisfying our palates with goodies that bring us comfort and satisfaction. My friends and I sitting around a table breaking bread together is far more than just having a meal; it's the true form of peace talks, a common thread that we can all agree on, "I'm hungry. Feed me."

I grew up with a mom and a dad and a brother, in a home where the four of us had family meals often, sitting around the table at the same time for the sole purpose of eating and sharing the events of our day. Since there were no such things as cell phones, Twitter, or other social media, if no one spoke, we were left with the sounds of forks clinking on the plates. It was a natural and relaxed opportunity for my parents to "interrogate" my brother and me. As Dad cut his pork chop into bite-size pieces, he asked, "So, did you get your score on your math test today?" Of course, he already had received the intel from Mom. But it was his way of prompting me to discuss whatever was on my mind, and I did.

We did have one telephone that hung on the wall in the kitchen. It was a party line, so when we picked up the receiver, we often found people already talking. I got whacked many times for listening in instead of immediately hanging up. The phone rarely rang during meal times because decent people would have never been so rude. But if it did ring during supper, it continued to ring.

We were not late for supper. "This is not a diner," Mom would say. When the food was ready, we ate. There were no microwaves for individual warm-ups. This must all seem unimaginable to today's younger crowd. But that was our reality, and it was wonderful. In looking back on my childhood memories, those where we were around that table, laughing, crying, and eating are always the ones most prevalent. In those moments, all became right with the world. Things hard to face were discussed, common emotions of the day were shared, and a bunch of separate happenings merged into one collective memory we all created.

In contrast, my first chow hall experience in prison was a far cry from family meals back home. In single file, we were marched in, then picked up a tray at the window and sat where we were told to sit. No time to waste on chit-chat because eight minutes later, we were marched right back out. When a prison has two thousand men to feed, there are not many options about the process. But I was determined to find a way to create a family-type supper even in prison, at least occasionally.

Luckily, the prison had a commissary where we could order various food items once a week. One of the most popular items was Ramen noodles—ten packages for a dollar. And since I was only making seventeen cents an hour working in prison, bargain shopping was a necessity. I began with a Saturday night supper when the chow hall menu called for the basic slop. That week, three inmates in my cell block and I each had ordered a few commissary items that I'd use to prepare our Saturday night supper. My menu: Ramen Noodle Casserole, Apple Salad, and Pop-Tart Cake (don't ask). Compared to what was being served in the chow hall that night, this was a gourmet meal.

The four of us looked forward all week to our Saturday night meal. I spent the week making paper plates out of cracker boxes and gathering contraband ingredients from around the prison. In the unit, I set the table, served the food, and we all laughed and talked and shared our day's events. It was the one thing that brought us together—the equalizer, a shared meal. Many such suppers have occurred over my twenty years in prison. My recipes have grown, and my guest lists have changed, but each supper has been an event where walls were let down and friendships developed. It never failed that curious folks walked by our table and commented. Usually they wanted to know how they could be included. It was a good thing.

I discovered that my supper mates and I had more in common than we ever imagined. Sharing a meal allowed us to drop the bravado and the layers of emotional protection we placed around us and simply exist as human beings who needed to eat. As a result, we found ourselves greeting as we passed by each other and smiling occasionally even in the midst of the coldness and steel of prison. Slowly a community formed, and it became my prison family.

Good things seem to quickly end in prison because of the transient nature of the population and the unpredictability of being indiscriminately moved from one facility to another. The general motto is, "It's good till it's not." So some inmates find themselves living in the moment and embracing the good happenings while others don't get involved and insulate themselves from continual grief over the loss of any goodness. I have been on both ends of that spectrum and must continually push myself to embrace life in the moment.

Recently, I found myself being transferred to a different prison with a reputation for violence and gang activity. I was placed in the absolute bloodiest unit that housed four top gang leaders and their cronies. Correctional officers were afraid to stay in the unit much of the time, allowing all 128 inmates to run wild and uncontrolled. My paleness stood out like a dove in a field of blackbirds. I saw the inmates eyeing my property packed up in a few clear garbage bags as I dragged it into the unit like fresh meat paraded before predators waiting for a new kill. I wondered if the theft of my property would involve my getting beaten up by a gang or stabbed with homemade shanks. Would I be raped in the process and left to die? I felt the certainty of violence of some kind—when, where, and how were the only unknown details.

I walked into an empty cell. The previous occupants had just been taken to the hole for stabbing an older man for his commissary food and hygiene items. The cell was filthy with human waste still in the toilet and black soot still on the walls from burning cigarettes hand-rolled in Bible pages. Just behind me walked in a younger man, tall with imposing features, his clear bags of property in tow— my new cellee. The officer pushed the cell door shut because the prison was going on lockdown. So, there we were, two strangers in a nasty eight-by-ten–foot cell sizing each other up. I introduced myself, and he responded, "I'm 'Too Tall.' I'm a Crip, are you affiliated?" "No," I responded. He didn't look too surprised and was asking out of common prison courtesy. We each went about our business, putting stuff away on the rusty metal shelves and cleaning the best we could with a rag and a bar of Dial soap.

The roaches scurried about as we intruded on their spaces, the crevices found in the nooks and crannies around the room. No words were spoken; just two bodies moving about in a dance learned from years of occupying small spaces in prison.

By nightfall, only a flickering fluorescent bulb remained to light our space. I looked at the few commissary items I had left from the trip: a summer sausage, a bar of cheese, a pickle, a bottle of mustard, and a sleeve of crackers. I decided to open up all the items as I knew they would be stolen tomorrow if the lockdown lifted. I meticulously laid six crackers on two separate pieces of notebook paper. I tore the sausage and cheese into twelve pieces and did the same for the pickle. With a dab of mustard on each cracker, I stacked the ingredients to form the appetizers. My cellee lay silently on his bunk, never taking his eyes from my operation. "Too Tall, here, I made us some snacks," I said, as I handed him the paper lined with six meat-filled crackers. With a slight hesitation, he extended his hands and took the snacks and allowed a wrinkly smile to form in the corner of his mouth. The rest of the night, for hours and hours, we talked about our families, our pasts, and all those crazy prison stories we had accumulated over the years. Food became our common experience—a light-hearted and unpretentious moment to relax and be vulnerable and safe.

As it turned out, Too Tall was the enforcer for his gang. That title represents everything you may think it does. In fact, he had just returned from a stint in the hole for "enforcing" on a person who disrespected one of his gang brothers. When morning came, the lockdown was lifted, and Too Tall was quickly out of the cell. I sat on my bunk awaiting my fate. I looked around the small room to see what defense mechanisms I had available. I decided to hold a hardback book to try and stop any knives being thrust at me. Soon, Too Tall entered the cell and exclaimed, "You won't have any trouble. I told the brothers they would have to deal with me if they thought about doing anything stupid where you are concerned." And that was that. Sharing a few cracker snacks formed a bond of humanity between two people from very different worlds.

In this prison, I have found it more difficult to gather a party of convicts around a table to emulate my earlier experiences, but I have found various ways to open doors and create bonds using food as the equalizer. Simply sharing a homemade burrito or a sweet microwave creation with someone I found intimidating or threatening was my way of saying, "Hello, I care about you as a human being sharing this experience of prison with me, and I want you to be happy." And trust me—sharing a burrito is much less stressful than carrying around a shank for protection. Once I decided in my heart that violence was not an option for me, the decision to use something I loved as an olive branch seemed very clear. As Henri Nouwen once wrote, ". . . it is possible for men and women . . . to offer an open and hospitable space where strangers can cast off their strangeness and become our fellow human beings."[1]

I'm sure I did not make Mom and Dad proud by being in prison, but I did make them proud by continuing a custom of family and community at a place in great need of both. Perhaps before you start building a fence between you and your neighbor's house, try delivering a plate of cookies instead. Just lead with your heart. Extend your hand, even to the scary "cellee" in your own neighborhood. You may find your best friend as a result and someone who has your back when troubles loom.

When you take violence off the table as a remedy for the situation, you open up your mind to a vast array of other possibilities. It forces you to think outside the box in order to find peace and understanding. In an age where it seems easier to fire off some

1. Nouwen, *Reaching Out,* 65.

angry Twitter words, or in prison where it seems safer to carry a knife, why not decide that it's not easier or safer? Instead, find the humanity that is shared between the souls of everyone: "I'm hungry. Feed me. Love me."

Break Bread With Me ───────────────────

The goal is wildly audacious
In this place
Live in peace and not fear

The fear is like wrestling a bear
In this place
It's hard to shatter the precedent of violence

A meaningless existence surrounds one
without human connections
In this place
It's hard to pet a biting dog

It can be done with
resilient optimism for better
In this place
The need to oppose must disappear

Break bread with me
In this place
Enjoy this moment for there is no other

Don't look at our differences
In this place
Just look at our shared humanity

3

Cutting Through the Pain

I guess all people have defense mechanisms they use to protect their bodies and souls from pain and emotional damage. Prison forces you to develop layers of protection against all its inherent assaults. These walls, however, seem to erode the conscious mind of all feeling, creating a zombie land of half-alive beings unfocused on their surroundings or circumstances. Some inmates eventually find constructive ways to bring some of their emotion to the surface in order to test the temperature above water. These prisoners may stay surfaced for a while, or they may descend to even greater depths to further insulate themselves from devastating emotional pain.

Sometimes the pain itself seems the only way a person can know he is alive. Bodies with scars of self-mutilation move about the prison, their wounds representing their desire to feel—anything. Blood flowing from a fresh cut relieves the pain trapped inside and allows the acknowledgment of at least some life.

It's hard to comfort someone who is falling into emptiness. The end is darker than the beginning, and falling seems appropriate as the darkness blinds him to the pain. This is the case for Jeremy, whose life is a tragic example of pieces of a soul falling like raindrops on a windshield, dismissed as easily as wipers pushing them aside. In Jeremy's twenty-two years of life, he has suffered physical abuse, sexual abuse, and drug addiction. Worse still, he was living with a drug-addicted prostitute for a mother along with her revolving door of boyfriends who burned Jeremy's arms, legs, and genitals with their cigarettes, leaving still visible scars. Jeremy was on his own, and fending for himself eventually led him into criminal activity.

Although Jeremy has been in prison for only a few years, he has managed to get tattoos all over his exposed skin, even on his face and hands. Even among the hardened old heads who have been in prison for years and years, the tatted skeletons and demons painted over his body make Jeremy an intimidating figure. Little by little, tattoo by tattoo, Jeremy has covered himself, creating a shield from the senses and feelings of prison, a shell to protect his innards.

During my years in prison, the types of people I attract for conversation have changed. There is a certain beauty that comes with youth, but age brings on the beauty of the soul. Fragile people in prison seem to recognize, at times, the need to reach out for the wrinkly words of old heads, for a map to help find their way through the wilderness. So, at times, I feel like a travel agent attending to walk-in clients who happen to be inmates attempting to gauge the topography of prison. Most of these would greatly benefit from mental health services but must settle for dime-store words from other travelers who somehow managed the treacherous terrain of incarceration and lived to tell about it.

My first encounter with Jeremy was strange and familiar at the same time: strange in that I had never spoken to him before; familiar in that younger inmates gravitate towards me for advice. I saw his tatted face peering through my cell door and then heard him lightly tapping for permission to enter. Hesitantly, I motioned for him to come in, so he entered and sat down on the toilet, a common seat for visitors in the cell. I said nothing, waiting on him to begin the conversation. Awkwardly, we sat in silence for almost a minute until Jeremy lifted his head, revealing teary eyes and quivering lips. Then he said, "I always see you reading and writing down at the table and know you have an old prison number—you must be pretty smart?"

"I don't know how smart I am," I said, "but I am a good listener if you need to talk."

For the next two hours, Jeremy barely took a breath, gushing out his life's story like a faucet left wide open. I had seen it many times before, people needing to purge themselves of trauma, sin, pain, like confessing to a priest. The only real thing needed from me was my time and attention. Jeremy didn't expect me to fix him or judge him. He just needed me to listen to him and to recognize that he was alive and not invisible to the world.

Although I remained quiet, with an occasional nod of my head, I soon reached sensory overload. Dealing with my own emotional distress while taking on that of another human being was overwhelming, but seemed necessary in this moment. When Jeremy left my cell, the air was heavy with the baggage he left behind. I knew that I could not exist in such burdened space for long. So I soon began humming a song I sang in church many times:

> Amazing grace, how sweet the sound
>
> That saved a wretch like me
>
> I once was lost but now I'm found
>
> Was blind but now I see

And peace was restored.

Jeremy had shown me the many cut marks he had made with a razor blade on his arms, legs, and neck, not so deep as to need stitches, but deep enough to bring on blood and leave a scar. Each cut represented the release of built-up pressure in his soul that was about to explode. And each cut allowed him to remember that he was alive, still a part of the world. Soon, the pain was sought after, wanted, desired, addictive.

About six weeks after our visit, Jeremy cut his wrists deeply and nearly bled out, needing a life flight to the hospital. He survived and returned to the same prison, with his only mental health precaution being his promise to the staff that he would not try to kill himself again. A week later, I passed Jeremy going to chow. As he approached me, we locked eyes, and he allowed me to hear him say, "I know what to do next time." And walked on.

There is a lot of blame to go around regarding Jeremy's current condition. Some may say that he is an adult and must now face his own decisions and live with the consequences. But is it that easy? Can people who need mental health treatment heal themselves? Are self-inflicted incisions necessary to purge the pain trapped in a man's soul?

The Persian poet Rumi once penned, "Out beyond ideas of wrong doing and right doing, there is a field. I'll meet you there."[1] I want to meet Jeremy in that field, and there we can talk without judgment and acknowledge together that he is a valuable human being. We can affirm together that he is alive and deserving of so much more respect than he's ever known.

1. Quoted in Moyne and Barks, *Open Secret*, 8.

My c
o
c
o
o
n

I'm spinning
Methodically
Deliberately
With Constant Motion

My cocoon is forming
Thicker
Thicker

Soon it will be ready
A time for me to invert
A shell from the world
A protection from the hurt

Sounds are beginning to fade
Colors are blending into a pale grey

My cocoon is forming
Thicker
Thicker

The air is no longer brushing my hair
Smells, Tastes, Sounds
Now insignificant

It must be finished soon
or it will be too late

No one to rescue me
It's up to me
ALL ME

My cocoon
A home till a
m
e
t
a
m
o
r
p
h
o
s
i
s occurs

Stay With Me

DEATH why do you
torment me so
the tease of you looms
over me with great expectation
fear of your occurrence is
being replaced with
excited anxiousness
you have grown closer to me
I feel your breath on my neck
it brings me comfort
stay with me
you keep leaving
will you wait until the
darkness blends the land and sky
how do I make you
feel welcomed
I pray to see the blackness
of the space you inhabit
don't leave
stay with me

I feel your breath on my neck

4

Beyond the Living Room

I imagine that most people have times of regret and remorse in their lives and wonder how many things might have turned out differently if other roads had been traveled. Prison has a way of bringing an abundance of such people together, where that regret and remorse are as thick as sludge in a drain pipe. The nastiness of all the sins of the past has a way of building up until everything becomes blocked. Life ceases to have meaning, and any ability to produce anything positive seems impossible. The difficulty with many I interact with in prison is that their lives, from the very beginning, have been tragic and hopeless, perhaps because they missed out on a unique, biological family bond. A family can provide a means to fill that hole of hopelessness. Those who are unable to connect with their kin may well seek other family units—some good, some bad.

Some men around me in this concrete cage continue to live in the only manner they have ever known—destructively. Much of the destruction within these walls can be associated with gangs, which while not the only problem in prison, are the majority of the problem. The gang leaders understand they possess a lot of influence over fellow inmates, as well as over the prison administration. The list of negative actions by the gangs is endless, ranging from drug sales to murder and everything in between. Non-gang members quickly become victims, or what the gangs call "prizes." New gang bangers must earn their "street cred" by preying upon these "prizes." Much of the criminal activity waged by gang members is to increase the power of their collective family, their fellow gang members. So their victims become mere "casualties of war." Grieving over them is considered senseless and even a stain on the family.

As strange as it may be, I understand the family aspect of the gang culture. What would we do to protect or feed our family? Most of the gang members I've come to know were not raised in a traditional family unit. Some lived in neighborhoods that offered no sanctuary outside of the gang family, neighborhoods where prison was always seen as a future reality and a rite of passage—no if, ands, or buts about it. Such was the case for "Joe Cool," a high-ranking member of the Crips. He was young enough to have an entire future still ahead of him, but he was so entrenched in the gang family that more than likely his life would be shortened by some horrific, senseless activity of his group.

For many months, I had watched Joe Cool terrorize inmates around the unit where he made no bones about the fact that he would use force to get what he wanted. So I was quite surprised when I heard the unit officer tell Joe Cool to pack his stuff and roll out to intake. Joe Cool had completed his sentence and was leaving prison to return to his community, the same one where he began his lifetime membership in the Crips. I felt like a kid watching a three-ring circus where the anticipation of the high-wire artist falling to his death makes you look without blinking. Was it really possible that this violent creature was being allowed to walk out to the Free World?

Part of me was greatly relieved that the prime terrorist in the unit was leaving while another part shuddered at the prospect of his home community again being terrorized by his destructive activities. Had the taxpayers who funded Joe Cool's stint in prison gotten their money's worth? Had their dollars been spent rehabilitating Joe Cool or wasted by only warehousing him?

I was mesmerized at the going-away party staged by Joe Cool's gang family. Each member gave him slips of paper with names and addresses of people, not to pass on greetings, but to settle scores. Joe Cool's years of incarceration had apparently been a training ground for becoming a hit man. If the number of slips of paper were any indication, there were plenty of hits to be done. Joe Cool was going to extend his victimizing from prison to the Free World.

Joe Cool was like so many inmates who are warehoused for years without any legitimate treatment, counseling, training, or mentoring. He had been allowed to continue and even grow in stature within his gang, without being stopped by the system or shown a better way. I imagine that much of society sees the millions spent on corrections and assumes that much is done to rehabilitate prisoners. However, it's funny how plans often look good on paper but don't always translate well into reality.

Most people who visit prisons only view the "living room" and never go into the rest of the house to see the real deal. Growing up in the South, we all had living rooms. It was the room at the front of the house that was always clean and put together for good presentation. Of course, no real living took place in the living room as it was off limits unless special company was over. The orderly, maintained, polished room was the façade we hoped visitors would buy and accept, believing the rest of the house was just as spectacular. God forbid if visitors had to use the bathroom. Getting there would take them through a maze of toys, garbage, barking dogs, and an ironing board piled with wrinkled clothes. In other words, where and how we really lived.

Taxpayers mostly accept seeing the living rooms of prisons and never bother to peek into the real living space where the dirt and grime of life are actually found. If they did, they would see treatment programs that are unsuccessful and unhelpful; they would see education programs where apathetic teachers don't care if you learn or if you sleep at your desk; they would see roadblocks put up to keep Free World volunteers from coming in to help; they would see a staff mostly cowering to the demands of organized and destructive gangs, a staff who dread coming to work and worry about their own safety; they would hear the desperate cries from inmates who want to change, to find a new path, but can't find a source for help. The bloodiness and the deafening cries beyond the living room are not appropriate for company. But are taxpayers company? They own the house, don't they? It's possible the house may be condemned before any repairs are completed, the lives inside accepted as collateral damage. If left unattended, termites will eat the entire structure.

Today, I wonder about the victims Joe Cool has yet to create. If people had walked beyond the living room and had demanded the rest of the house be just as clean and organized, would Joe Cool have had a chance? Joe Cool entered prison burdened already with his own tragic circumstances. There, he found a hopelessly flawed system of incarceration. He leaves worse than when he entered, now with an agenda of violence. I wonder, will it ever be different?

> "To see what is in front of one's nose needs a constant struggle" (George Orwell).

I See a Home

I see a home for me
Whittled amongst the weathered wood
A crevice to rest my worn body
A place of solace to smell the sweet scents of freedom
A place for me to exist
One that you envisioned long before I did
There it is—just beyond the horizon
A cozy warmth from the mud-brick fireplace
The one you made, brick by brick, drying in the sun
A pot of stew smelling of pearled onions and rosemary
The one you made, cutting each piece of beef precisely even
A chair by the window draped with a beautiful quilt
The one you made, stitch by stitch, just for me
A door that swings both ways, no locks
The one you hung for me—never to be confined again

I see a home
Just for me

The one you made

5

The Art of Redemption

Developing a community and, ultimately, friendships requires extending to folks more than casual greetings, quick glances, or insincere nods. It takes asking sincere questions and waiting—*wanting*—to hear the answers. Not with any expectation of fixing someone's problem but as a means of letting the other person know, "I hear you and stand with you." Sharing our stories can help us find our common humanity and understand that we all have similar emotions. We all desire to be heard and loved.

During the twenty years of my incarceration, listening to stories from those in my community has helped me form meaningful and lasting relationships that extend beyond the fences to my friends who have been released or transferred to other prisons. Writing and receiving letters may be a lost art to those in the Free World, but to those in the penal system, letters are treasured jewels—tangible pieces of someone's heart, read with your eyes, felt with your hands, and smelled for fragrances of life on the other side of your existence. I could fill volumes with stories that reflect common emotions of regret, loss, grief, pain, and suffering from those inside these concrete walls. A story recently shared with me reveals all those emotions. It's Art's story, the story of his rocky road to redemption.

As confining and destructive as prison can be to its inhabitants, it's possible that some, paradoxically, are able to find new freedom behind these razor-wire fences. When those in the Free World face unrelenting stress and chaos eating them alive, even a cage can be welcomed solace, a place to lick your wounds and recover. What devastating events could happen in your life to totally change its trajectory? What level of desperation would it take to lead you to commit criminal acts you never imagined you'd do? Art's life exploded in a cataclysm of such events in 2008 when his health failed, his job was terminated, his family left him, and his wealthy lifestyle was destroyed. Now at age fifty-three, Art finds himself in prison, a place he never imagined he'd go.

A white, middle-aged, college graduate with professional credentials is not a typical prospect for incarceration. Nonetheless, here he sits with me in the cell we share, reflecting on the path that led him to prison. An intriguing sort, with a soft, blue-eyed gaze, gentle features, small frame, and a nonchalant stride, Art looks like the subject of "Finding Waldo" among the hardened, weathered souls surrounding him. His age, along with his ability to converse eloquently with prison peers, uniquely allows him to move about without much fear. Like a deer sighting a hunter, his wisdom, maturity, and experience warn him to leap away from danger. Even as harm lurks and presents itself daily from unwelcomed pursuers, Art has managed to maneuver around the hunters thus far, walking delicately through the frightening forest.

Art was born in a small Georgia town, where his mother became the most influential person in his life. He says of his mother: "Perfection was her ultimate goal. In her eyes, wealth and status equated to success and happiness." When his father left, Art's mother sat him down and told him he was never to speak of his father again, and he didn't. In a generation where children were to be seen and not heard, expressing himself or showing emotion was prohibited. It seemed his mother cared more about public perception than her children's feelings. So Art learned soon enough that the stories being formed inside his house were secret. In fact, Art said, "My first memory is having sex at age four with my uncle. He told me and I believed that his behavior was normal, but very secretive." I wondered if Art's mother knew anyway, and allowed it.

It didn't seem odd to Art to be one person at home and another out in society. I challenged Art when he said, "I loved having sex with my uncle." To me, it seemed unnatural for Art to suggest that what was happening was sex and not abuse or rape, but Art pushed back. He explained, "Those moments made me feel special, wanted, and loved. I really didn't know what was happening. All I knew was that I felt good when we had those times. When it ended, years later, I missed them."

Because of his mother and his uncle, Art traveled a path he had been taught was normal. Decent people go to school, get a job, get married, have children, and keep their secrets buried deep. After all, what would people think if you varied the course? So each day, Art got in his upscale car, drove to his upscale job, and acted in his upscale life, following his mother's Hollywood script, performing the only acceptable role.

In 1997, while going through marriage counseling, Art wrote a letter as part of his counseling homework. The goal was to write down painful secrets and seek forgiveness. Art's wife found the unfinished letter a few weeks before the next counseling session, and during an argument, she revealed that she knew his secret—Art was gay. That day was the first time Art said out loud, "I'm gay." His life changed drastically from that point on.

Amazingly, after some emotionally rough years, Art managed to find a way to communicate amicably with his three children, and even with his ex-wife, and to experience some happiness. One layer of the onion had been peeled away, and Art was able to imagine finding a new role, playing his authentic self. Even though Art's mother now knew the truth regarding his sexuality, she struggled to accept it. Still vitally important to her was what people would think, especially about her. Clinging to the idolatry of "perfection," she drifted back into society where she had spent a lifetime building a "perfect house," brick by brick, using theater clay that did not withstand the dramas of life.

When Art's brother became an addict and his health began to deteriorate, Art offered his home as a sanctuary. Their mother even came there to live and nurse her "favorite son" back to health. But it was not to be. He died, and that was that. Shortly thereafter, Art's mother said to him, "I was ready for you to die, but not him." Her pointed words pierced Art's heart, confirming what he had known for a long time but tried not to admit, at least not out loud: he was a failure in his mother's eyes. It was then he heard again words his mother told a guest at his college graduation. When told how proud she must be of Art's accomplishment, his mother replied, "I wish it had been his brother graduating because he had the smarts to be a doctor."

In 2008, life threw Art a curve ball he could not catch. In fact, it hit him smack in the head, knocking him into uncertainty about how his upscale lifestyle would continue. That year, after being diagnosed with HIV, cancer, and shingles, Art was unable to work, and he was put on short-term, and eventually long-term, disability. His reduced income could no longer support living in his prestigious neighborhood, driving his fancy car, or even paying for his expensive, life-sustaining medicines. The layers of the onion were pulled back, revealing a vulnerable mess of a man unable to cope with all the garbage life had heaped upon him.

Some years earlier, while on business travel, Art had experimented with meth. He remembered the temporary escape from reality that the drug produced and longed for a few more such moments. There it was—a new friend who didn't ask questions, didn't judge, and was always predictable. Art was not an addict and understood soon enough that meth was not the answer to his emotional needs, but it did offer some possibilities for his financial needs. Selling meth yielded the income he needed to prevent total catastrophe.

This choice, however, was the one that brought him to prison and also the one that may have saved his life. There is no pretense in prison. Prison is not prejudiced; wealthy socialites can be stabbed and raped as easily as the crack heads. Regardless of background, inmates become indistinguishable, blending into the concrete structure with look-a-like costumes and emotionless expressions. No one is better or worse; you are just a number, marked, tagged, and tracked forever.

Being thrown into the deep, dark pit of prison can become a reality check on life for anyone. At the bottom of that pit, finding any light at all requires an almost impossibly steep climb. Facing that climb is often too much to bear, so you sit at the bottom, feeling your heart beat, and hearing your own breath. The dirt and the worms around you seem like a spa mud pack, exfoliating your skin to expose the raw, tender, true meat beneath. You sit there until you begin to realize that the fall into the pit has not killed you—you are alive.

In his pit, Art's eyes were opened to how hard but how necessary it was for his survival to scale that wall and shed the harm done to him by his family. He learned that a common bloodline does not make a loving family. He learned that freeing ourselves from destruction is harder when the devastation is caused by blood-kin. He learned that sometimes our kin need to be swatted away like a mosquito whose bite can infect our souls with nasty germs. He learned that sometimes it is better to make a new family, the best kind, one chosen, not born into. With great effort, Art did all of that. Because Art climbed the steep walls of the pit, he can now see light, real light, brilliant light, for the very first time.

Art and I spend hours sharing stories, laughing, eating together, and asking each other, "How are you doing—for real?" By choice, he and I have become part of a new family for each other. However, Art will soon be released from prison, and then he will embrace his life with new awareness and new determination to live authentically. He will live in a world seen with new eyes, a world where he can live marvelously—fully himself, truly redeemed.

The Perfect House

It looks good from a distance.
But secrets are held inside.
The ground is shaky.
The house was built on lies.
The dwellers seem All American,
until you open the hidden door.
It shakes the foundation.
The truth must be released—even if
the perfect house is demolished.
Sometimes, it's better to tear it down and
start from scratch.
Some things can't be repaired.

6

A Little Kindness

"Do your little bit of good where you are; it's those little bits of good put together that overwhelm the world."— Desmond Tutu

Prison has a way of concentrating a bunch of negative energy such that it becomes routine to see and experience the worst in people, both inmates and staff. Staff members (or "the Man") are usually so apathetic about their duties and the inmates so broken down by the system of justice that neither group seems to indulge in kind conversation or acts of compassion. So when unexpected kindness or compassion does occur, like a large wave rushing to shore, the news spreads quickly among those in the cell block, leaving the inmates awestruck. Sometimes you don't know what's *wrong* until you see what's *right*.

This year Christmas lacked even the limited excitement usually found in anticipating each bite of a good meal—real turkey and a piece of pie. The Department of Correction decided to eliminate special holiday meals for all prisons in the state, so whatever food was on the regular menu would be our Christmas dinner. Bah humbug! Most of us spent the day watching television and calling family members, wishing we were with them around the tree, seeing their faces as they opened presents. Holidays are especially grueling for inmates because each occasion is a tough reminder that our mistakes separate us from our loved ones. These special days raise our awareness of the difficulty we have in feeling forgiven by God, by others, and especially, by ourselves. So when you least expect it, if even a little kindness is poured upon you,

you melt into life and love with a new hope, a new outlook, and perhaps a renewed belief in God's love and your own humanity. A recent experience brought this to light:

Date: Christmas Eve

Time: 10:15 PM

Setting: Prison, Unit 9, all 128 inmates locked in their cells for the night.

Scene: Third-shift prison guard enters from prison door left to begin shift. Female, early fifties, red hair, never worked this post before.

As they naturally do, many inmates are looking out their cell door windows to see what guard is taking post. It's good to know who is in charge of your life through the night in case an emergency arises. A guard with bright-red hair takes a big plastic bag, full of something, from her large tote-bag. She carries the bag as she begins her first round of cell checks for the night. Beginning in a soft whisper and gradually amplifying to a full, clear voice, she begins singing in tender, melodic tones: "Silent Night, Holy Night / All is calm, all is bright . . ."

The inmates who were not peering out their doors at first are all now looking at this woman singing a Christmas song. As she approaches each cell, she takes two candy canes from her bag and, smiling but not speaking, she slides them under the cell door. She continues to sing, delivering candy canes and smiling until she passes all sixty-four cells. By the last leg of her route, all the inmates join her in singing the Christmas carol: "Silent Night, Holy Night / All is calm, all is bright . . ."

The red-haired angel blessed us with love and kindness and left our hearts calm and ready for sleep. Many inmates ate their peppermint treats immediately, but some, like me, laid them on the bed as poignant evidence that we had not dreamed the entire event. I'm still holding on to mine.

Endless Love

Love knows no boundaries.
It defies all human logic.
It pays no attention to what the world thinks is okay.
It cares less about the obstacles that stand in the way.
It doesn't care how long it takes or how hopeless
the situation seems.
If it is meant to be, there will always be a way.
And with you, God, the possibilities are endless.
Show me how to love and to be loved.

7

Sentenced To Death: By Old Age

When a horrific crime occurs in this country, prosecutors frequently seek the most severe punishment. A perpetrator of such crime often comes to prison with a death sentence. That prisoner may be executed by a variety of means, like electrocution or lethal injection. In such cases, there are strong constitutionally mandated safeguards to ensure that, despite the severe crime, the felon is protected from the agony of "cruel" or "unusual" punishment.

However, for others, whose lesser crimes are found deserving of what are intended to be lesser punishments, there may be sentences of life in prison or even shorter prison sentences that are often retributively extended by repeated denial of parole pleas. For these offenders, the resulting punishment—a long, slow, and painful aging and dying in prison—is often far less humane and far more cruel than even the death penalty. Frequently, lifers face the reality that "bare biological life is all that is left, in which one may be killed without being either sacrificed (because not being a person of value, one's death demands no ritual) or murdered (because one's death has no legal significance)."[1]

Because the full reality of this supposedly lesser punishment is not explicitly handed down by a jury or pronounced by a judge, because it occurs in shadows behind prison walls, because it occurs gradually over many years, it is rarely vetted for compliance with protective constitutional mandates. How ironic it is that the long

1. Dolovich, "Creating the Permanent Prisoner," in Ogletree and Sarat, *Life*, 109.

"lesser" sentences often become the cruelest and most unusual punishments of all: "Death: by Old Age," lived out in prison.

My prison sentence is "Life, with the Possibility of Parole." In Tennessee, the current interpretation of this sentence requires that I serve fifty-one years before I am eligible for parole consideration. Since I am already in my mid-fifties, this essentially means I will die in prison. A recently filed challenge to this interpretation of the law could possibly reduce the number of years required not only for me but also for a few thousand other inmates in Tennessee prisons. But, at this time, change seems merely a hope and a prayer. At this point in my life, death in prison seems more likely than eventual freedom from these wire fences and steel doors. Even though I accepted this fact long ago, the court challenge generates a range of emotions for me to deal with. Should I allow myself to hope that I could be released from prison one day, or should I remain in my emotional safe space, accepting my eventual death in prison?

Death seems to loom over prison like thunder clouds in a rain forest. I have seen death up close many times during my years of incarceration. When someone dies in prison, the push to resume normal activity soon follows. Anything interfering with chow or rec is an unwanted intrusion and is quickly swept aside to get back to the routine. For example, I remember when Howard dropped dead while jogging in the rec yard one day. Other inmates were more disturbed about their rec time being cut short than by one in the community dying. I was astonished at the cold lack of emotion displayed at a moment deserving of sympathy and reverence.

Death in prison most often is impersonal and odd. Perhaps this is so because paying too much attention to it would force us to examine our own mortality. Who wants to do that? Facing personal mortality is frightening, especially when a big razor-wire fence separates us from the people who love and care about us.

In 2012, the ACLU reported that the number of older inmates in prison is increasing; accordingly, the number of deaths is increasing. Many of these old inmates have not been explicitly given a death sentence, but they will die before ever being freed and given an opportunity to reconnect with their loved ones. Walking around prisons are elderly inmates whom you would normally see at a nursing home. A 2012 ACLU report estimates that by 2030, there will be more than 400,000 prisoners who are fifty-five or older, compared to about 9,000 in 1981.[2]

Inmates live under a constant state of stress, receive poor health care and nutrition, have limited physical activity, and are at higher risk of injury and assault. This leaves elderly prisoners especially weakened and vulnerable to the victimization and abuse of inmate predators and helps to explain that "an incarcerated person's physiological age may exceed his or her chronological age."[3] When trying to guess a fellow inmate's age, I find it is best to subtract about ten years from the age suggested by his appearance.

Whatever the reason, prison ages you. I remember the first time someone addressed me as "Old School," and I was only in my forties. I turned around to see who he was referring to, only to realize it was me. It's rare that you know each other's real name in prison. A nickname or other term is usually used to address or call-out to someone. It's just the nature of the place and provides yet another level of the impersonal fog necessary to survive. "Old School" is a term used to call to an older person or someone who has done a lot of time. So when I was first addressed in this manner, it took me back a bit. Yes, my remaining hair has turned gray, wrinkles have developed on my face, and I've lost some of that zip in my step. But "Old School" did seem a bit much. It was quite a shock.

For me, each day in this place is now a fight. I fight to stay alive, trying to get my blood pressure medicine that Medical may or may not have in stock, trying to find space to move around and stay active, trying to stay out of harm's way, trying to fight the depression that sneaks in through every possible opening. But some days I wonder why. Lewis E. Lawes, warden of New York's Sing Sing Prison in the 1920s, said this about the emotional toll a life sentence takes: "Death fades into insignificance when compared with life imprisonment. To spend each night in

2. ACLU, "At America's Expense," i.
3. Chiu, "It's About Time," 5.

jail, day after day, year after year, gazing at the bars and longing for freedom, is indeed expiation."[4]

I often wonder why I should wait for my body to give out, leaving me incapable of helping myself. Many times I've seen inmates get transferred to a special needs facility where the isolation and confinement are so intense they wish for death.

> Elderly prisoners who need advanced medical care complain that they are being transferred to special skilled nursing units that are akin to solitary confinement. In these units, they are denied visits from fellow inmates, many of whom are like surrogate family members after many years they have spent together in prison. They are also prohibited from leaving the unit to attend programs and religious services and to use the library. Some elderly and infirm inmates are refusing treatment or are not seeking medical attention so as to avoid facing the end of their days isolated and alone in one of these special units.[5]

I witnessed this up close when a friend in my unit was dying of cancer. Bill had gone through rigorous but unsuccessful medical treatment. Before receiving each treatment, he had to pack and store all his property and ride the chain bus to a distant prison hospital. The chain bus ride is so traumatic that it often deters inmates from seeking needed treatment. After being handcuffed, shackled, and waist-chained to restrict arm movement, an inmate is placed on a hard bench right up against another inmate. The rows of seating are so close together he cannot move his legs. Bus rides often take four to six hours. The inmate is not allowed to exit the bus for any reason until the final destination is reached. Without bathroom breaks, many arrive at the destination suffering the discomfort and humiliation of soiled and wet pants.

The bus ride only amplifies the pain and misery those seeking medical help are already feeling. Imagine having a herniated disk in your back, while traveling to get an X-ray—restricted by chains,

4. Lawes, "Why I Changed My Mind," quoted in Ogletree and Sarat, *Life*, 75.

5. Gottschalk, *Caught*, 172.

sitting on a hard seat, and having no leg room. Imagine, like Bill, having to do all that while weak from cancer, nauseous, and unable to access a toilet for four to six hours. Is this not cruel and unusual punishment?

After the treatment, Bill had to suffer through the additional misery of waiting seven to ten days to get back to his originating facility. These boring days were spent in an isolation cell without any of his property, without even a book to read. After another grueling chain bus ride back to his home prison, it wasn't unusual for some of his stored property to be lost or stolen in his absence. All the while, he was in great pain as his organs were shutting down.

Bill's cellmate tried to care for him, even changing his bed linens after he lost control of his bladder or worse. Bill could have received more pain medicine, but not without being housed in the infirmary, having no contact with fellow inmates, no TV, no books—nothing. Bill chose to stay in his cell, bear the pain, and die among the people he knew, who at least cared for him. Bill died in his cell, holding the hand of the chaplain and with familiar faces around him. Believe it or not, in prison, that is a pleasant death and not one prisoners usually experience. Bill was blessed.

Any inmate who is forced or agrees to go to a special needs facility or stay in the prison infirmary is walking into an existence devoid of human contact or compassion. It's a lonely and tragic way to grow older and die. Many of these elderly are not serving a life sentence but often will die in prison because their bodies give out before their sentences do.

So, where does that leave me? Even if Tennessee changes its interpretation of a life sentence to require fewer than fifty-one mandatory years, I doubt I will live long enough for public opinion to change on this issue. This means that I will most likely never be granted parole. As much as I would love to catch hold of some ray of hope, it seems foolish for me to do so. My time may be best served by trying to live—truly live—the best life that I possibly can right here, in the place I am. For me, that means talking and writing about issues and emotions associated with living in this place. I write because, if treatment of the incarcerated is ever going to become less cruel, people will need to look inside these fences, see the living conditions, hear the life stories, and understand that prisoners are human beings. I can help with that.

I Shall Not Die Alone

If today becomes my last moment on earth,
I shall not die alone.
I will not hear the whispers of hope
muttered from a stranger.
I will not seek comfort from a preacher
whom I've never met.
But I will remember the eyes that have looked into
mine with love and inspiration.
Drifting through my mind will be words that
have uplifted me—the real me.
The one not bridled with deception and fear.
I will feel the touches of those who
were not afraid to reach out to an
outcast of the world.
If today is my last day, I don't need
medical folk simply doing their job.
I just need to remember.
Remember the words of my God.
Remember the love of my friends.

I shall not die alone.

Maybe Tonight

It's hard to watch the sun go down knowing that another
    day has come and gone.
Maybe tonight will be the one where I slip into the arms
    of God—comforted, loved and secure.
Maybe tonight I'll trade this old body in for the soul that
    lingers beneath.
Maybe tonight I'll cry my last tear for the sins of my past.
Maybe tonight the memories that haunt me will become
    a forgotten past.
Maybe tonight I'll bow before my king and embrace the
    majesty of a future undeserved but given by grace.
Maybe tonight.

8

Monsters Don't Live Under the Bed

As a child, I could never find a peaceful sleep until I looked under the bed to ensure there were no monsters. You know the kind—those creepy, scaly, red-eyed devils waiting to eat your brains as soon as you doze off. When I turned double digits, I decided I was too old to be scared of fictitious figures like Santa Claus, the Easter Bunny, and, most importantly, monsters under the bed. But prison has revealed some of those long lost monsters. Turns out they are not under the bed but hiding in plain sight, right in the midst of us.

I have met the most incredible people in prison—real friends who have become family to me. Many have been released from prison and still remain close and in contact with me. But there is evil in this place that I have also observed up close for twenty years. I've seen people in this culture stabbed, killed, molested, and bullied. Blood was spattered on my clothes as a man was nearly killed right at my feet. Evil lurks with uncomfortable closeness.

I would be careless not to recognize that many in society would label me an evil person, even a monster, because I have taken innocent lives. On the surface, it would be difficult to argue against that assumption. I have heard many victims and family and friends of victims suggest that those convicted deserve all the bad things that may befall them, perhaps even the death penalty. I don't want to discount the reality that most people in prison have left a multitude of victims on the other side of the fence. Those victims are understandably entitled to all the grief and anger resulting from their victimization and toward the perpetrators who harmed them.

I have certainly accepted the fact that I deserve to be in prison. I also believe that forgiveness and redemption are possible for even the worst of the worst. I can strive to be better, do better, and work at being a child of God who helps humankind—even prisoners. Going forward in my life in a positive way does not remove the remorse and sorrow I continually feel for the victims of my crime, nor does it come with any expectation of forgiveness from the broken hearts left behind. But I do believe forgiveness comes from God when you humble yourself before him and seek it.

Prison is simply a microcosm of the larger society, filled with those who are working to do no more harm, those who harm unintentionally, and those who actively seek to do harm. Prison simply puts all of that right up in your face with no way around it. Prison rule number one says that a convict should not see, hear, or act on anything that does not personally involve him. Trying to follow this rule has been a continuing moral dilemma throughout my incarceration. Watching even a stranger being abused and not calling for help or helping myself is an incredible struggle of conscience. My heart is burdened with the fact that I have mostly followed the rule out of fear and trying to fit into the culture. It has been reinforced through seeing those who did get involved harmed or killed. It is simply a lack of courage that I remain ashamed of.

In addition to the larger society, prison is also similar to family life in significant ways. For example, when a little boy misbehaves, a parent may send him to his room, away from the rest of the family, for a time to contemplate his wrong-doing. The parent knows the child's room is safe and close, just in case. Because the separation creates a great void for both the family and the child, the parent's goal is to welcome the child back into the family fold as quickly as possible. But imagine if the child's window had been left opened and evil crawled through it and harmed the child. The child might never be able to recover, might never trust his parents again. This would truly be a tragedy.

When a person comes to prison, the State is his official guardian. The State is simply a mass of people; therefore, the people of the State are the prisoner's guardians. The people send one of their own away to prison for a time to contemplate his wrong-doing. Are the people's intentions to receive the inmate back into the fold as quickly as possible or to keep him in prison as long as possible? Do the people try to prevent evil from getting to the one who is outcast, or do they turn a blind eye and allow the inmate to suffer all possible punishment? Such retribution may hinder the inmate's ability to trust other people. This could easily block his recovery and ability to live productively once released from prison. This, too, would truly be a tragedy.

In both scenarios, there is a child, someone's child who is yearning for a safe place and a chance to rejoin those he loves as quickly as possible. How will his loved ones find him when he does—remorseful and wanting to do better, broken and forever wounded, or extremely angry and resentful as a result of his separation from the family?

Unlike the young child, many behind the fence have no hope of a hero running in to rescue them from the monsters. Some reach out for a way to cope with the isolation, loneliness, and other monsters creeping round the concrete walls. Many times that means drugs. Drug addiction is one of the ugly monsters in prison. Fortunately, I don't have such an addiction and have never taken part in that side of the darkness that inhabits prison. Through the years though, I've seen many people battle the monster of addiction and fail when left to their own devices. Amazingly, drugs are as available in prison as they are on the street. It's a dirty business. It is made worse by the gangs who run it and prey on the vulnerable and the addicted. Not long ago, when my new cellmate arrived, I saw firsthand how the drug monster shows his ugly head.

James seemed nice enough at first glance. He shook my hand and began the ritual of getting acquainted as new cellees do. I noticed that he did not have a television, radio, commissary food and supplies, or anything of real value, as he placed his property on the metal shelves. "Stolen," he said, explaining why he had no property, which didn't seem too far-fetched in this environment. All seemed well between us. Less than two days in, James found a drug connection, and the monster slowly revealed himself. In the next several weeks, the drugs became more present and their effects more severe. When he found a rig (a homemade pump with an attached needle to inject drugs into the vein), all hell broke loose. James was always high on something. One night, however, the injection of some hyped-up drug allowed the monster to totally come out of the shadows.

I had grown accustomed to James staying up most of the night, fiddling about, and sleeping most of the day. So each night about ten o'clock, I put in my earbuds and listened to music to drown out the various noises. This particular night was no different until I was awakened with the weight of a sweaty, naked man on top of me. I was startled at James's glazed eyes as he stared into mine. My hands were trapped under the blanket with James pinning me down with his body: a large white man, at least my size, in his late thirties, and in full monster mode.

He forced his mouth onto mine, pushing his tongue into my throat. The putrid taste of tobacco and bad breath almost made me hurl a gush of vomit. I bit his tongue as my only defense, and he quickly removed it and jumped off of me, slurring a flood of profanity.

"What the hell are you doing?" I yelled.

"You know you want it, you bitch," he responded. He soon had me in a head lock, and I felt my blood gushing through my head veins, my eyes forming that tunnel vision that precedes blackout. And then it was black.

When I was coming around, I felt James trying to enter me but not having much success. I pushed him off of me, and he did not fight back. He raised his arms in the air as if to surrender and said, "Fuck you then—I'll get off by myself." And he did, standing by the toilet.

After that, he got into his bunk, went to sleep, and that was that. I did not go back to sleep. I brushed my teeth, washed myself, sat on my bunk, and silently repeated over and over, "Be still and know that I am God." I found myself rocking back and forth in true disbelief about what had just happened.

I was out of the room as soon as the morning officer unlocked my cell door. I phoned my Free World friend and heard the voice of love, gladly realizing that there was still some good in my life. It was a strange day. James eventually woke up and began to move about. All he said about the incident was, "Man that was some crazy shit I shot last night. I hope I didn't keep you up all night acting crazy—man, I can't do that no more." And again, that was that. My nights no longer included listening to the radio while falling asleep. Instead, I lay with my back to the wall, listening for James to fall asleep before settling into a night's rest.

Prison is full of stories like that and much worse. I thought that I had gotten too old and gray to worry about such behavior, but the drug monster thought otherwise. And then there is that old prison rule number one, which must be applied even to attacks against me. Telling officials would have only gotten James and me both locked up in solitary for seven to ten days, while most of our property would have been stolen. After the prison's "investigation" (meaning nothing), we would have been released back into the world of the unknown—with a new cellee who may have had his own monsters to reveal. Even worse, my prison reputation would then be that of a "snitch," the worst thing you can be in here. I decided to deal with the monster I knew rather than face a new crop. I told you I was not very courageous.

Yes, evil crawled through my prison window. This monster was a real one. Will I learn to trust again? Can I let go of my fear? Is recovery possible? Living in a state of fear robs life of all joy and makes it impossible to see any good in your path. A dear friend and yogi sent me a wonderful book. Healing words from this book were the first I read the morning after: "Fear is the only obstacle to joy. In the moment you let go of fear, joy is present."[1]

I must let go of fear and open my eyes to the love given to me by the kind people who are willing to see past my evil deeds, past my own time as a monster, and embrace the person I've become.

Although I was fortunate to have a few resources to help me cope, many others are not so fortunate. I remember Kenny, a nineteen-year-old entering prison for the first time, getting off the chain bus in clear view of the rec yard where a bunch of us were

1. Schreiber, *Child of Existence*, 188.

standing and watching. Having been in prison only a short time myself, this ritual was both fascinating and disturbing to me. As the newbies walked off the bus one at a time, old-head predators were making rude and obnoxious cat calls. As they spotted their potential victims, they were hollering out: "Fresh meat," "Young stuff," "My new bitch."

Kenny's clean-cut, young image did not serve him well in the prison environment. Within a few weeks, Kenny had been passed around by the predators for sexual pleasure, like a cheap prostitute. I saw his physical image change drastically, becoming that of a weary, glassy-eyed zombie. When Kenny fought back one day, the predators attacked him with unspeakable cruelty, causing permanent damage to his genitals. After he was taken to the hospital, we never saw Kenny again. I imagine he was eventually taken to another prison. And thus began my life of seeing and ignoring. Part of me was relieved that it wasn't me, and the other part felt guilty for remaining silent, for my lack of courage. For Kenny, the monsters were in plain sight. Inmates and staff alike turned their eyes away, protecting themselves, while allowing the weakest to be brutalized.

There are many others like Kenny in prison, but there aren't many David and Goliath stories these days. Individuals feel small in the face of such mighty monsters. But when a village comes together, slinging stones at Goliath becomes possible. Will society, now knowing that evil awaits, continue to leave its children's bedroom windows open? Or, can we unite and find enough courage to face the monster and speak out? Can the loving family of humanity embrace its children and assure them that monsters are not permitted in any child's home?

> Now I lay me down to sleep
> I pray the Lord my soul to keep
> If I should die before I wake
> I pray the Lord my soul to take

> God bless Mommy, and Daddy, and all my friends
> And please don't let the monster get me.

In Those Moments

It happens occasionally
Someone just extends her hand
It catches you off guard
It is not a normal occurrence
But it happens
When you least expect it
A smile, a letter, a card, a kind word
Just when you need it
God presenting himself to us
Through his beloved creatures
In those moments
Those very special moments
We touch the hand of God
And feel his love, compassion, and forgiveness
In those moments
Everything is okay
The strength to go on exists
A miracle
That is what it is
God loving us
That is what it is
And even though we recognize it only occasionally
I'm sure it happens often
Miracle moments

Taking Flight

I'm floating above my body.
I'm aware that soon I'll need to
    melt back into the shape of skin
    and bones that
        feels
        cries
        hurts
But for now, I've taken flight
    above the sorrows and hardships
    of life to be free from
        pain
        emotion
        suffering
I'm lingering in order to experience every
    moment possible,
    to just be still
    to just be
    to just
    to
I'm back.
As soon as I embrace thought, I'm
    doomed to return to the shell of life.
I'm already thinking of my next moment
    of nothingness.
It's the place I find God.
Each time, he is waiting for my arrival
"I've missed you"
        And all is well.

9

Buster

Buster was an ornery sort, full of piss and vinegar, with a rough, weathered, and worn outer layer formed by decades of hard living in prison. Buster was the inmate clerk for the unit manager at the prison I had been transferred to. I often saw him moving around the unit, tending to the business of the pod, but I kept my distance from his unpleasant disposition. I needed to ask him a question about mail one day but quickly changed my mind when I heard him cuss out another inmate for asking what Buster considered a "stupid question."

One day, I was caught off guard when I saw Buster hurriedly making his way toward me with a steady gait and his eyes locked on mine. "So, you're from Clarksville?" he asked. It seems he and I were born and raised, ten years apart, in the same small Tennessee town. We both still knew all the old haunts and gathering places of our generation.

Soon we found ourselves laughing and carrying on like two old classmates at their fortieth reunion. Often we would be standing in the chow line waiting to pick up our tray of gruel from the serving window and imagining we were going to Moss's Café, a historic meat-and-three back home in Clarksville. "Today, I'll have the BBQ, mashed taters, stewed tomatoes, and green beans," he would say. "In that case, I'll get the beef, corn, turnip greens, and okra," I would add. Of course, both plates would have included Moss's famous cornbread sticks with fresh butter for smearing. We always let out a disappointed sigh as we approached the window and got a glance at the unknown substance on the tray. "Maybe tomorrow," one of us would always say.

It didn't take me long to realize that Buster's crusty old exterior and pickled personality were just a disguise. I discovered that Buster's heart was loving, generous, and sentimental about sharing his kindness with others. Yet, years of experiencing the pain of disappointing responses from other inmates had left him with an outer shell of protection that, at first contact, was not easily cracked. I understand the need for many inmates to develop such a shell. Getting attached to a friend and suddenly having him or yourself transferred to another prison feels like your family is being ripped apart—and, in prison, it happens over and over again. Eventually, you avoid developing any friendships in fear of the heartache that always follows.

Each week Buster listed extra ramen noodle soups and soaps on his commissary order. He placed these items in small brown bags so that when newbies moved into the unit with nothing more than their state-issued prison blues, he could present them with a "brown-bag special." He always told the newbies, "This is from all the guys in the unit," never taking personal credit. He told me the reason for his generosity. "I know how it is to be new and scared in this hell hole. It's not much, only a few soups to fill your gut and soap to wash your ass, but it means a lot when you have nothing." Along with the brown-bag special, Buster made sure the newbies also had a sheet and a pillow, both highly coveted items in prison.

I don't know what brought Buster to prison. Asking convicts such questions can be detrimental to your health, so inmates don't ask. It really doesn't matter anyway because all I needed to know was that whatever wrong Buster had done already had cost him years and years of prison time.

Not long after I met Buster, he was diagnosed with kidney cancer and had one of his kidneys removed. When he returned from the hospital just days after his surgery, he was weak and frightened but still had some degree of optimism about getting back to normal, getting back to work. But the next few weeks of throwing up and pain left Buster exhausted and thin. Soon he was so thin that his floppy skin seemed draped over a mere bag of bones. With his pace slowed and his head down, his once confident steps gave way to creeping about with a slow shuffle.

We got news that all the inmates at our all-male prison were going to be transferred to other prisons in order to make room for a growing female inmate population. Not knowing when this would happen or where we would all go enveloped us in a dark cloud of dread and fear. One night at 1 AM, about thirty of us were abruptly awakened by military-styled officers and told to put our stuff into one plastic garbage bag per inmate. If it didn't fit in the bag, we couldn't take it. Dazed, I tried to get my senses about me. We only had fifteen minutes to pack our belongings. I started making two stacks on the floor: my absolute needs, and things I would leave behind. All my books and most of my commissary items had to stay. My clothes, hygiene items, and my writings, I could pack.

Looking in the cell window, the guard yelled "strip," a command you quickly become accustomed to in this place. Whenever you move to another location, you are always strip-searched. Standing in front of another person totally naked, you are told to open your mouth, hold up your arms, and lift your sack. You are then turned around and told to bend over, spread your butt cheeks, and cough. Then, after the guard searches your clothes, he tosses them on the floor at your feet for you to put back on your body.

Dragging that garbage bag full of only my most needed possessions felt like running out of a burning house, only having time to grab what you can't live without. It's hard to do. I was already having regrets about not looking through the books I left behind— for hidden treasures of letters I would often keep between their pages. Those were letters that I needed to read over and over to remind myself that there are people who love me. Too late. No turning back. Handcuffed and shackled, I was marched to a prison bus and separated from my bag of belongings. I wondered if I would ever see my only worldly possessions again.

As I stepped into the bus, there was Buster, hands and feet chained, already sitting on the small, hard plastic bench. Snot dripped from his nose. A puddle of vomit curdled at his feet. He, too, had been herded into this bus load of transfers. I managed to sit behind him and spoke to him, trying to get a response. But he didn't turn around or lift his head. He sat quietly in his own despair. After six non-stop hours traveling in the bus, we finally arrived at our destination, the new prison location where this bus load of convicts would now be housed.

Marched off the bus one at a time, then unchained and stripped again, we all were brought into a large room where our garbage bags were piled up and we were told to find our items. It was a frenzy of pushing and shoving, each trying to retrieve his "life-in-a-bag." Many of the bags had been ripped open and contents tossed around, lost forever. I found mine and pulled it over to where Buster stood, gazing at all the aggressive activity. "Buster, where's your stuff?" I asked. Buster managed only to shrug his shoulders and shake his head. By then, there were just two bags left on the floor. I brought both over to Buster. All he could do was point to the one that was his. And that was that.

Buster and I were sent to the same unit but to different cells. The cells had recently been vacated by rival gangs after a knife fight. Blood was still on the cell floors and walls. The guard allowed me to help Buster put his few items on the shelf. I was also allowed to find him another pair of pants as he had thoroughly wet his during the long bus ride. After he lay down on his bunk, I felt okay about leaving him to go to my cell to tend to my own unpacking.

Slowly, Buster regained some strength, began to talk again, and even managed to crack a smile occasionally. Talking about our shared Clarksville experiences always revived his fond memories, and I could tell he had hope again. I thought of Victor Frankl, a concentration camp survivor who recounted the words of Nietzsche: "He who has a *why* to live for can bear almost any *how*."[1] It seems that, at any level of human existence, life really has no meaning if there is nothing to hope for. For Buster, simply thinking of returning one day to a place he so loved was enough for him to reach for life and not give up. Although our *whys* for living may change hundreds of time over our span on earth, I believe every

1. Frankl, *Man's Search*, 76.

one of us must hold on to at least one of those *whys* in order to open our eyes and face this world another day.

Not long into our stay at our new place of confinement, Buster's health went downhill again. After several trips to the prison medical clinic and a hospital visit, Buster was diagnosed with bone cancer. This, in addition to the kidney problems, colostomy, and hepatitis C he already had, seemed to exhaust any hope Buster had of seeing Clarksville again. He knew it, and I knew it.

He was prescribed pills to slow down the cancer, pain medication, and something to help his nausea. Unfortunately, despite the dose schedule specified on Buster's prescriptions, medications were dispensed one dose at a time at the prison pill window only three times a day. So all through the night lockdowns, his pain and nausea were his cross to bear. When he did get his meds, doing so required him to walk the distance of a football field from his unit to the med window and back. He was almost too weak to make the journey or to endure the often one-hour wait in the long pill line.

I was not allowed to get his meds for him, but, when I was able, I would make the trip with him. We would stop along the way for him to rest his hands on my shoulder and catch his breath. To reduce the awkwardness of this pause for Buster, I would point out the skunks roaming the yard, as I questioned their purpose for "visiting" our prison. I would also call Buster's attention to the birds scooping up bread crumbs thrown about by inmates returning from chow. Often the yard officers would yell out "hurry along, no stopping," ignoring the weakness of an old man, only noticing that he was wearing prison blues. Buster would comment, "Sorry bastard, he'll be old one day."

Buster became desperate as his condition worsened. He knew he needed to be transferred to another city where the only prison hospital in this state is located. Our prison only had a small clinic with a few short-term cells to control those on suicide watch or having psychotic episodes. The clinic was not equipped for long-term medical patients. Buster knew that the financial aspects of the contract between the state and the private company managing our prison made transferring him to the state prison hospital very unlikely.

So Buster asked me to help him write and file a formal grievance, officially registering his complaint about the lack of adequate care he was receiving. This was a desperate move.

Filing a grievance often results in retaliation against the inmate who files it. When a grievance is filed, the named department must supply an answer to the complainant, in hope of resolving the matter. This procedure was established years ago when federal measures were taken to reduce prison violence in our state. Officials realized that when bad things are happening to inmates who have no voice, the result is often violence and even death. A grievance procedure was established to provide a means to get problems resolved before they escalated into violence. If done in the correct spirit, it can be an effective tool. However, recently, complaining about anything at the prison is considered hostile and unruly behavior. As a result, instead of resolving the issue, negative measures are often taken to hush the inmate. So, for most inmates, filing a grievance is so risky that it usually is done only as a last resort.

After I helped Buster file his grievance, soon enough his fear of retaliation was validated. Instead of finding a way to make meds more accessible to Buster in his unit, the medical director decided to move Buster to a medical clinic cell. This was the worst possible outcome of his grievance. It would leave Buster sick while in a situation of virtual solitary confinement: no television, no radio, no visitors, no friends, just isolation, a punishment for asking for help. Just Buster with his cancer, now waiting for death, all alone.

The unit officer told Buster to pack his stuff. He only had fifteen minutes to get his belongings to the medical clinic cell, so I helped Buster pack his things. Once again, we crammed his property into a garbage bag while silently glancing at each other, knowing what was ahead. Buster's fragile body was pale and weak and broken. He seemed like an animal caught in a trap, just waiting for death. I didn't want Buster to see my own unstoppable tears because I feared he would sense the doom I was feeling. Buster shook hands, saying goodbye to his buddies in the unit, no longer caring to conceal the tears that rolled down his cheeks. I walked with him to the medical clinic where a small, cold room was to be his last home, his death chamber—a lonely casket that closes on you while you're still breathing.

As I was quickly rushed out of the clinic to return to my unit, I looked back to catch one more glimpse of my friend. Our eyes locked, and we exchanged gentle smiles, knowing this would be the last time we would ever see each other. Walking back to my unit, I was filled with anger and guilt, feeling responsible for putting Buster in this predicament. He had come to me in such desperation, in great need of help and relief. It seemed that through my words written on a piece of paper and sent as a plea for mercy, I had only helped him to his prison death-room. It seemed that the very people who should have valued Buster's human life did not. Buster had given me his sister's name and telephone number in case something happened to him. I got word to his sister to let her know about Buster's condition and situation. You see, even in matters of life and death, prison officials don't alert friends and family to an inmate's declining health condition. An inmate is allowed to designate one person who will get a call only when the dead body is ready to be retrieved from the morgue. Until then, the inmate is considered the property of the state and nothing more—like a slave on a plantation, traded back and forth as commercial goods. Buster's sister called the warden, the chaplain, and the medical director, only to be told nothing—she had no right to know that her brother was dying.

My heart breaks over Buster's situation. And, as much as I grieve over Buster, I also fear my own dying process in prison. I walked through this process with Buster, as I have with others before him. The fight to receive medical care in prison is an exhausting struggle. In the end, the fight you wage is usually rewarded with solitary medical isolation—a means to silence you while projecting to the world that you are under "constant medical care." So this lump I recently found in my armpit and the irregularly shaped and discolored spot that is on my left side present a daunting dilemma for me. If I were in the Free World, I would immediately seek medical evaluation, diagnosis, and, if needed, treatment. But in prison, the fight to get these concerns addressed is a fight I cannot emotionally bear to wage. I could not bear the isolation that is risked by complaining, asking, or even begging for care—that same isolation that was Buster's cruel fate.

To most, it would seem that only a simple decision was needed to send Buster to a hospital. Hello! SOS! He's dying now. There's not time for weeks and weeks of emails, unreturned phone calls, and clawing up the chain of command. Is a simple, humane response to an obvious, immediate health crisis too much to ask? But prison administrators often seem paralyzed by miles of red tape that seem long enough to stretch to the sun and back. Why is no one willing to take charge of fixing this obvious problem? Is it just too big to deal with? Is it a budget issue? Does compassionate care for a dying Buster cost too much to justify? Does no one want to look into Buster's eyes and see that he is a human being—a living, breathing child of God? Could it be that recognizing the humanity of this inmate and then doing nothing would be a weight on the conscience that could not be carried? Does remaining impersonal keep one safe and free from blame or responsibility? What price is paid for taking the easier route of seeing Buster's prison-blue uniform and caring only to know his prison number?

What I do know is how sad I feel that my friend is in pain and dying and that his last days have been unnecessarily difficult physically and emotionally only because basic human compassion was denied him. I am sad that I am not allowed to visit with him and help care for him. I will miss Buster.

Perhaps on the other side of the mountain, Buster and I will meet at Moss's Café and share a plate of warm corn sticks. Until then, my friend, may you rest in peace.

My hands touched God's hands today —————

He was tired, sick, discouraged
Helpless, he was, and hot with fever
But he was God, and I knew it
Did others not see the glow of
    angels' wings all around?
I placed ice cubes on his lips
    and fed him chicken broth
Could others not feel his holiness?
I realized the only reason I recognized
    God was my closeness to him,
      unafraid and thankful to be at his feet.

Once a Slave . . . Always a Slave? ──────────

I've been marked today
Branded as a slave to the state
Right there, on my right wrist
A plastic band clamped with metal clasps

> *Itchy*
>> *Sweaty*
>>> *Pulling at my arm hairs*

A constant reminder that: I'M PROPERTY

Send me where you wish, Master
I'll avert my eyes from yours as you walk by—as you directed
Cause eye contact will make you remember
                    Remember that you are my slave master
Will you recollect these eyes when I am your neighbor?
Will you then greet me—acknowledge my presence?
Or will you still avert your eyes—so as not to remember
                    Remember that you were my slave master

I've been marked today
Branded as a slave to the state
Will this harsh treatment keep me from returning to this HELL?
Or will it break my ability to ever TRUST or INTEGRATE into
the world?
You have the power—given by whom?
Is your ego stroked when you put me on the block for display?

> "Look at my obedient slave—I've broken him
> from wrong-doin."

Will you recollect these wounds when you see me at Walmart?
Will you greet me—acknowledge my presence?
Or will you still announce to the passersby:

"Look at my obedient slave—look at his wrists—the imprint is still there."

"HE'S NOTHING"
"HE'S WORTHLESS"

10

Is It Just This?

"Abandon all hope, ye who enter here." A sign bearing these words was at the entrance of the Tennessee State Prison that opened in 1898. I would imagine the statement was the first clue as to what awaited the inmates walking into that intimidating, cold, stone structure. But, with most inmates returning to the Free World eventually, is hope really what you want them to give up?

I've spent a lot of time thinking about hope and what exactly it means, especially because I use the word every day in some manner: I hope you are well, I hope things work out, I hope your pain is better, I hope I get out of prison, I hope . . .

Without consulting Webster, I challenged myself to define "hope" in ten words or less. This proved to be a greater chore than I imagined. Eventually I came up with this: "Hope: a mysterious expectation that things will go a certain way." I chose to use *mysterious* because I often hope for something to happen that has no logical basis. Perhaps, this comes from my belief in God and from my knowing there is much I don't understand. I guess that hope and prayer are pretty much the same thing since I often ask God to do things that require a power greater than I possess. So, "I hope you feel better," and "Please God, heal my friend," are basically the same thing. In essence, all through the day, I find myself saying these little prayers, or extensions of hope, for myself and others. Does this even matter? Yes, having hope is essential to life. Without it, there is nothing more, no way out, no relief from pain, no end to misery—it is just this.

I often encounter inmates who say they have given up hope on so many things—occasionally, even on everything. With no hope, often they wither away into depression or get hooked on drugs, taking them down a self-destructive rabbit hole. My own hope seems to flow like the sea, in waves, with low and high tides that take sand back out into the water to be lost in the deep darkness at the bottom. Violent acts around me erode some of my hope, but on those days when I close my eyes and realize no one has died today, including myself, I wake up with sandy eyes looking on the day anew. Through all the craziness of my life, I have never lost all hope. I've always seen some glimmer of light shining through the cracks of my brokenness.

Occasionally, I am encouraged by seeing hope displayed around me:

I see Charlie, who has written his children each week for eight years with no response. He hopes they know how much he loves them.

I see Carlos, who has been studying for three years trying to pass the GED test. He hopes that, when he gets out in eight months, the certificate will help him with job prospects.

I see Mr. Neely, seventy-four years old, with crippling arthritis, pushing his walker around the unit each morning, trying to strengthen his bones. He hopes, after being denied parole three times, that this time up, he will be able to join the ranks of those in the Free World.

I see Freddie writing letters to halfway houses. He hopes to find a place that will accept him and waive the initial fee, for he has no money or support.

I see countless others who each day wake up and bow to a system that seems to want to keep them chained up instead of free. They hope that one day, society will give them a chance to be a part of the world again.

The idea that inmates should "abandon all hope" seems a cruel and unnecessary message for people just cast out from society, just separated from their families and friends, and just put in a cage to waste away. Perhaps a more useful sign would read:

Have hope, all who enter here.

You are alive.

Change and redemption are possible.

Such words could provide the dark souls entering prison some light to find a path away from the feelings of worthlessness and unforgiveness that weigh them down. It takes time, a lot of bandages, and much treatment to overcome the damage done to the weary bones entering the prison warehouse. There is no triage station at the prison door to put inmates in the appropriate treatment line, just a room, many rooms, for new "patients" to move about and re-wound each other. Those entering prison will always be permanently scarred by the harm they did to the victims of their crimes. Those scars will continually remind inmates why they have been separated from the world. Perhaps it is a rightful separation, a time to reflect on the harm done and a time to repair the brokenness that led them down dark paths. Healing is possible if they learn to treat their own wounds and suture their own jagged pieces together. The system is all talk and no do at the repair stations. But one thing must remain if any such repairs can be successful: hope.

In my many years behind the razor wire, much has changed in my life. Seeing my child change from boy to man, my hair from black to gray, my body from young to old, my possible years of life from many to few, my heart from cold to warm, my tears from few to many, and my words from lies to truth—my world has gotten smaller, my time on earth shorter, but I still have hope. I have hope because I have breath, and I have God who can mysteriously make my expectations come true. Even if it is just this—forever—I still need hope and prayers for the strength to bear it.

If you should enter these gates one day, shield your eyes from that sign. Do not abandon all hope. Instead, know that each day you are alive, there is always another chance, there is always that mysterious expectation.

There is always hope.

Is It Just This? ——————————————————————

There is no end in sight
All roads have ended
    No directions posted

There is no game plan
    No strategy
    No bright idea
    of what to do
    or how to do it

Is it just this:
    LOST

There is no hero
    No white knight
    No savior
    to come and carry
    me to safety

Is it just this:
    HOPELESS

Stop thinking
Keep breathing
Be quiet

Is it just this:
    PEACE

If it is just this
It must be okay
This must be happiness
    JUST THIS

it's not what i imagined

this day i woke up in a steel cage
surrounded by a bunch of strange people
have i been shipwrecked on an island
or am i still dreaming in my sleep
should i get out of this bunk
and face whatever awaits
or should i turn over, close my eyes
and pray for more sleep

sleep won't come

moving about on new territory
trying to get my sea legs
on this rocky boat

I must be steady
cause sharks are looming
waiting, watching for vulnerability

i'll survive
i always do
at least i have a history

but must it always start out
so difficult

it's not what i imagined my life would be

11

Wheelchairs, Walkers, and Wishes

I began the day as usual—when the prison is not on lockdown, that is—walking in circles around the unit. I call it "getting on the hamster wheel." With limited outside rec at this particular prison, walking is one of the few options available for exercise. I was relaxed, pleasantly trapped in my meditative thought as I circled and circled, stepped and stepped, looked and looked, until I began counting the wheelchairs and walkers parked outside the cell doors, waiting to be used by their owners. I counted four wheelchairs and two walkers. My first response was overwhelming gratitude that I was still able to move about without such devices, but my second response was sudden and startling—fear. My heart sank, realizing that if I die in prison, as my life sentence predicts, I will more than likely face disability, inactivity, and immobility. In other words, one day, I too will likely need those devices.

I got a peek into my possible future as I spent my day observing those with wheelchairs, walkers, and canes, noticing how they managed their activities. A few of those inmates seemed to be relatively independent, rolling about on their own or shuffling their walkers or canes steadily on the concrete floors. But one particular wheelchair remained parked outside cell number six all day long, without ever being moved or used. Since I was a rather new resident to the unit, I didn't know all the inhabitants of each cell, so I didn't question anyone. The next morning, while on my morning stroll on the hamster wheel, there sat that same wheelchair, still unused. My curiosity got the best of me, so on my next trip around, I stopped by cell number six and tapped lightly on the window. The door was unlocked, only pushed to, so I opened it a bit, stuck my head in, and saw a man lying on the bunk with his blanket covering everything except the bald spot on the top of his head.

"Hello," I said, as I stepped into the room a foot or two. "What?" the man screamed out. This startled me even though I knew I had just entered his room without appropriate invitation, an action convicts consider highly disrespectful and possibly aggressive in nature. In this setting, the two words spoken between us had already communicated volumes. I had signaled my approach to his person, and he, in turn, acknowledged me. No surprise that his tone indicated he was not at all pleased with my invasion. I tried to explain, "Sir, I was just concerned a bit. I haven't seen you about and was wondering if you're okay?"

He responded in a much more subdued tone, "Would you help me? I'll pay you."

"What sort of help do you need, sir?"

He went on to explain to me that his cellee had left a few days ago to make an outside court appearance and was supposed to already be back. "I've been paying my cellee a bag of commissary coffee each week to help me get in and out of my wheelchair, to the toilet, and with other things."

"What's your name?" I asked.

"They call me Rabbit cause my wife said I was as quick as a rabbit in the sack. Figured I could walk around ashamed of it or claim it and deal with it. Must not have been too bad—got six kids," he said with a slight grin.

I let out a little chuckle. He then pulled the blanket down from his body, revealing skin as yellow as a summer squash and eyes of brown set into pools of mustard. Turns out, Rabbit's liver had shut down, and he had become quite jaundiced and weak. He was still unrecovered from heart bypass surgery just a year ago, leaving him greatly dependent on a wheelchair. I knew his days were numbered. I told Rabbit, "I'll be glad to help you till your cellee comes back from court, but I don't need any payment. I'd love to hear more stories about your life." I understood why Rabbit didn't want to call attention to his need for help by letting an officer know. Doing so would have meant being sent to and permanently housed in the infirmary where the cold steel walls and loneliness were worse than solitary confinement.

Getting Rabbit moved from his bunk and from his soiled wet sheets and clothes was a challenging and pitiful situation. I had never cared for a person in that manner and wasn't even sure I was capable. Each time I looked into Rabbit's brown eyes, I could only imagine myself being in a similar state one day and wondered if anyone would be willing to help me and if I would be able to pay him for the assistance. What about the other 126 men in the unit who probably knew Rabbit much better than I did? Why hadn't they checked on him? Is it possible that we are all so caught up in making our own way that we keep others distanced and end up alone in a box we created for ourselves? It seems to me that living in community with each other is important wherever you are, prison or not.

As I helped Rabbit over the next few days, I marveled at the changes in him: desperateness and hopelessness changed to steadiness and hopefulness. We performed the bathroom duties—completing them without explanation or embarrassment. I pushed Rabbit around the unit and saw him interact with others, smiling, telling tall tales, and laughing. Each time he released a big belly laugh, he held his chest, still hurting from the heart surgery. With just a little bit of care, Rabbit sprang to life like a newly planted seedling getting a few raindrops and piercing its way through the hard soil. So much life was still there for Rabbit to enjoy, though not without the aid of a friend.

When his cellee returned, I became Rabbit's backup helper. I often think about the stories Rabbit told with such gusto and optimism. "I can't wait to get to that old pond and catch one of those big old catfish," he said over and over. I always smiled and nodded, even as I knew his was only a tragically lovely story. I hoped for his wish to come true but knew that his failing health and many years yet to serve in prison would prevent such an outing from ever becoming a reality. I would like to think that if

Rabbit were freed, his six children would care for him, allowing him to have the best quality of life possible. I don't know if that could happen, but what I do know is that Rabbit is right here, right now, needing a community to step up and honor life—the life left in him—a community of friendship willing to offer selfless service to the very end.

Meeting Rabbit didn't offer me much comfort for my fears about how my life in prison may end up. However, it did change my grandiose image of dying surrounded by all the people who love me, to a more simple wish: that someone, anyone, will be there to help me with the basic tasks of life, that I will not have to live out my final days and hours in the cold solitude of the infirmary. Even these basic wishes come with a large emotional price tag. They will require an investment of myself in my prison community where just chattering about the weather doesn't connect me with others. I will need to make myself vulnerable by sharing my fears, disappointments, hopes, and joys with my prison mates in order to develop relationships and, maybe, even lasting friendships. It seems ironic that the ups and downs of life's long journey all boil down to such a simple wish: to have someone close to assist with our most basic bodily needs. I suppose that old Irish proverb is correct, "It is in the shelter of each other that the people live."

Walk On

It is never what it seems
There is always more to the story
We render immediate judgments
But we really don't know

What is his story
That is the real question
But it takes too much time to uncover
So we really don't know

He just wasn't born so "whatever"
What were the paths he chose
This is part of his story
Too little time to know

So walk on, my friend
If you stop, you will unveil
The mystery of his person
The fact that he is human

Don't ask any questions
You may discover his torment
The tragedy and sorrows of his life
The fact that he is human

Walk on dear friend
Once you see, hear, understand
You will no longer be able to deny
The fact that he is human

12

Say No to Photoshopping

More than thirty years ago, as I waited at the end of that long church aisle to exchange wedding vows with the only girl I had ever dated, I never anticipated society accepting into the fold of humanity the gay man I actually was. But society would un-knowingly accept the photoshopped image of me. The fear that my true identity might be exposed often pushed me into a mental darkroom. In the small southern town where I lived, having a serious conversation about such an inflammatory issue seemed far-fetched at best. But times, they are a changing—and thank God for it.

The concept of photoshopping images may be a relatively recent technology; however, it seems I've been photoshopping my own self-image for fifty years. A schoolmate notices my sensitivity and calls me a "crybaby," so I tweak on that image to change my outward appearance into something different from what's going on inside. My Wonder Woman lunchbox brings on "homo," so it becomes a Superman lunchbox. On and on, until the outside looks nothing like the inside.

Ironically, in my thirties I entered prison, a place where people easily see through corrupted images and get to the nitty gritty of it all. In prison, there was nowhere to hide and no dark-room to work on the photos of the life I wished to present to the public. It was a reality check. Straight Tony became gay Tony, and the world didn't fall apart. In fact, it never blinked an eye. My place of confinement became my liberator. Gone were the decep-tion and manipulation previously necessary to maintain my ruse of straightdom. Unfortunately, society didn't change its attitudes with digital speed to meet my immediate needs. Change develops, it seems, in waves, spurred by incremental shifts in public awareness and sentiment.

Such was the case with civil rights, feminism, and now sexual identity. It begins when certain terms and ideas become politically incorrect to voice in open conversation. Some race terminology is banned from decent conversation, but those thoughts may remain heavily ingrained in one's worldview. Similarly, such terms have been stamped out from acceptable conversation when it comes to sexuality: "homo," "faggot," etc. But just because we have edited our words and photoshopped our images, our underlying negative attitudes are not instantly removed. That takes time—a long time. That change can only occur by getting to know each other in personal, one-to-one relationships. Understanding leads to tolerance; tolerance opens the door to acceptance.

The shift in public opinion usually doesn't come with an "ah ha" moment or a spontaneous desire to be more accepting. Rather, it comes with personal and intimate awareness: "My son is gay; my daughter has a girlfriend; my toddler identifies as a girl." You get slapped in the face and forced to look at how you want your loved one treated by the world. When you get comfortable seeing the real, unfiltered version of a person, it allows you to connect through shared humanness. Seen through such a panoramic lens, the differences begin to diminish, and then the shift begins, from marginalizing to accepting. It's personal.

Dietrich Bonhoeffer, in his *Letters and Papers from Prison*, reminds us that what is required to get a true reflection of a nation's character is: "to see the great events of world history from below, from the perspective of the outcast, the suspects, the maltreated, the powerless, the oppressed, the reviled—in short, from the perspective of those who suffer."[1] So, how the "least of these" are treated in this "Christian" nation would seem to be important. The outcast are certainly abundant in prison. In prison, being gay is the least of my worries. With me are brothers who range from

1. Bonhoeffer, *Letters and Papers*, 17.

mentally ill to serial rapists. Many different circumstances may have brought us to prison, but once here, we are forever the reviled of our nation. If ever released, we forever wear the scarlet letter of "felon" like a ball and chain clearly noticeable to all. So many who are released from prison begin the Photoshop phenomenon all over again. Prison tattoos and scars are covered with long sleeves; deep-burned memories of isolation and loneliness are concealed with audacious and risky behavior that many times results in rein-carceration. Trying to fit into a mold that society deems acceptable is unnatural, frustrating, and stressful—not meant for the faint of heart. Shuttering yourself within a false identity can wear you down like a continually resharpened pencil that is eventually left with only an eraser—an eraser now needed to remove the fake, photoshopped image you created.

To see a man love another man freely and openly out in the world is beautiful. However, many people still feel disgust. Same-sex couples holding hands while walking down the street or pub-licly displaying affection still brings about the "oh my God" and "look at that" sort of remarks. But these are the brave couples—the ones that help to shape history—the Rosa Parks of this generation.

I have learned that being authentic in prison also takes a courage of its own. The thought of persisting in prison with a complete photoshopped version of myself seemed a more ex-hausting endeavor than I was willing to continue. So, as in the Free World, the prison world also hosts gay, bi, and trans people, as well as all others along the spectrum of sexuality. Unlike the Free World, prison does not allow you to get in your car and drive to another community for a fresh start. Like it or not, what and who you are is front and center. Unless you develop thick skin, weakness prevails, and you are swept into the quicksand of life in protective custody. In prison, all are on the same side of the railroad tracks where truth is either revealed willingly or coerced by others. I have found that saying, "Hello people, this is me, like it or not" is both liberating and terrifying.

Thirty-some years ago I should have been saying, "I take you to be my husband" instead of "wife." But for so long the veils of my deception were worn like a shell of protection. I could not summon the courage to face my reality and certainly could not express it openly. As a result, the tragedy that brought me to prison followed.

Today, I believe that such tragedies, born of social rejection, are slowly becoming a thing of the past. Our nation is becoming a better place now that the road to social acceptance has been paved by such courageous people. Now men and women can live their lives with authenticity. Isn't that what makes life worth living anyway?

Reality Monster

Reality is a peculiar monster
    it must be faced
     whatever the fear may be

The monster can be avoided
   for a time . . . maybe

Different paths may skirt the monster
   for a time . . . maybe

IGNORING
   for a time
   the ugliness that awaits

But It Does Await

More time may be needed
    to prepare your brain
    for the fight

But the fight is your fight
    a one-man army

The monster is devious and manipulative
Years of maneuvers and practice
It knows all your weaknesses
    all your insecurities

His arrow is sharply aimed at your
    Achilles heel

When ready
    TURN
    WALK boldly toward the monster
    DON'T BLINK
    DROP your veil and say

"Hello monster
    Kiss my Ass"

Then surrender to his embrace

13

Hanging On in Tandem

Have you ever been in a room full of people and still felt lonely? I have and I do. When you take a person from his village and relocate him to an island where all the inhabitants move about in mysterious ways and communicate in strange languages, loneliness can certainly be expected. When I cautiously walked down those few bus steps with my legs shackled and my wrists cuffed and chained to my waist and stepped foot on prison concrete for the first time, I entered a strange world where fear, violence, and loneliness smacked me right in the face. I soon learned that it was impossible to run into my own arms for solace or comfort. I had to wait, hoping one day to find human arms stretched out to accept me, the real me, the unfiltered, flawed me. I didn't need a hero to protect me or even change my destiny. What I needed was someone to enter the emotional pit with me and simply remind me to "hang on."

Certainly, I have been privileged to make many friends during these twenty years of incarceration, most of whom, were fellow inmates struggling along with me to navigate the treacherous prison system. Such friendships are wonderful, but the loss of them can be emotionally devastating because inmates, like herds of cattle, are frequently moved to different fields when the system needs new workers. Without warning, your best friend can be suddenly gone, moved to another prison, leaving your heart bruised and anxious about getting too close to anyone else again. Without friends, it's nearly impossible to unload all the crap of the day. So you go on, and carry all the baggage yourself, until it's so heavy that something has to give.

I've had some good friends get out of prison and go on to have great lives in the Free World. However, as much as we may have talked about always staying close and in touch, it's never really the same. The Free World presents those friends with new problems and circumstances. For them to continue thinking about their lives in prison becomes too burdensome. They forget the emotions and feelings of this place. I guess we all have a way of forgetting pain—if not, how many women would ever have a second child? I don't blame my formerly incarcerated friends. They deserve to be happy and successful outside these walls.

I never expected God to save me from prison. My free will, my actions, created this destiny, and so, here I am in a place I deserve to be. But, even in the midst of my life in prison, God has ways of showing me how much I am loved: his words, the other humans he sends to me, the scenes of beauty outside my prison window. These are not meant to free me from my prison cell, but rather to linger along with me, share the space, and help me to realize I'm not alone in the struggle.

Some say, "As long as you have God you need no one else," but I don't agree. Certainly I need God; I always have. I've told God many times that I need more than his spirit, his words, or my thoughts of heaven. We don't need lots of people, or even a few people, but we do need at least one person with whom we can open up our hearts. I don't understand how anyone in solitary confinement for months and months, or even a person alone in a cabin for a long stretch, doesn't go crazy. I believe that one of the most magnificent ways we experience God is through other people, and so I asked for someone special in my life. I prayed for it, I expected it. And, after waiting twenty years, I finally found it through a prison pen pal program, with a lady named Cindy. Right there, in the midst of all that razor wire and steel, God sent me a portion of his unconditional love and forgiveness, in human form, a person who talked with me, listened to me, cared about me, and wrote me letters. At last, there was someone to jump into the emotional pit with me, not to save me, but to simply be, be with me, living in tandem with me.

After a difficult transition to a yet another new prison, I fell to the bottom of that emotional pit. During that time, Cindy and I began writing a tandem poem where each of us would write a line, mail it to the other, and so forth. Through the many months of my severe despair, this process allowed a few words to release the heavy heart-baggage I carried. Each verse lightened my load until, at the end, I knew that all I needed to do was simply hang on, just one more moment.

That's what a tandem friend, a true friend, does. She does not solve your problems but sits with you in the midst of your struggles. God was there, using his human creation to remind me that, even in prison, "I am here with you, don't be afraid."

Breathe—for *now* is not your *forever*.

Hang On

The pain knocks from the inside, for me to feel, others to ignore
It cries for attention, relief, solace, others not to hear
A heart smothered in unnatural darkness, facing a
    meaningless existence
A soul grasping for meaning, gasping for hope.

The air is stale, tarnished with blood and sweat from life's
    moments
The sounds, anguished and grating, mangled with repression
    and rage
Life has lost its sweet flavor, replaced with the bitter taste from
    words of disapproval and disappointment.

Yet, Love's faint remnants refuse to die, bringing life-giving
    salt to my sea of despair
Glimpses of tender memories tunnel through my brokenness
    to provide a mosaic of light to my soul
A light of sustenance, creating a shelter within
    when hell explodes before my very eyes
The light also brings awareness to the cracks in my foundation,
    forcing me to face the reality of things hidden
    in the shadows
My rose-colored foundation now fractured by realities
    of corruption, violence, cruelty,
        injustice, and just plain meanness against God's beloved.

An occasional ray of hope peers through the brokenness
    allowing my heart to pump blood for one more beat . . .
    one more beat
Saying, "hang on . . . hang on . . .
      hang on to sanity . . .
        hang on to life . . .
          one more moment . . .
            just one more moment . . .
              breathe—for now is not
                your forever."

Tony Vick and Cindy Ford
May to November, 2015

Tony Vick (center), with John and Cindy Ford. Holiday Dinner,
Riverbend Maximum Security Institute, Nashville, TN, 11/28/12.

14

It Is Possible

After only a few months in prison, I picked up my Christmas food tray from the chow hall window and, lo and behold, found a sliver of pumpkin pie. It was a lovely sight on a tray filled with watery instant potatoes and a paper-thin slice of bologna still icy from the freezer. A good southern boy would never eat dessert first, so I tried to swallow down enough of the potatoes to take the hunger edge off, saving the pie for last. I looked away for only a split second but immediately realized that my pie was gone. A gang member sitting at a nearby table had grabbed it from my tray and crammed it in his mouth. My memory of that Christmas dinner will always be of him, sitting there grinning at me, with pie crumbs falling down his chin.

I must admit this episode nearly made me cry. It would take me years to understand why. So many strong emotions were all provoked at the same time during that meal: I was angry at the audacity of the thief; I was ashamed that I did or said nothing to retaliate; I was disappointed that I didn't get to eat the pie; and I was embarrassed by the laughter from all those who witnessed the deed. I had not noticed at the time that the other inmates, before taking a seat at the table, had already eaten their pie. They knew that failing to do so would have made them vulnerable to being robbed, as I was. Years went by before I got an opportunity to taste pumpkin pie again.

My first cellee, Randall, told me something after that incident that I really didn't understand at the time. "Embrace and experience the good because it will soon be gone, and you don't want to miss it." Randall had already been in prison a decade and a half when I met him. He was a large man, six foot two, 270 pounds, all muscle. Up close and all too often, he had experienced prison riots, stabbings, and death. Randall had entered prison as a very young man, a high school graduate, but with tough-as-nails street smarts that served him well on the inside. For years he gambled, fought, did drugs, and spit on the system that locked him away. But when I met him, he had already begun his transformation. While in prison, he had earned a college degree in psychology through a government program. In fact, he had participated in every program and taken every class that offered help. He wanted to live differently, even though still in the cage of prison.

Randall had earned the respect of the gang leaders through his ability to reason through and mediate difficult situations. He became the "Switzerland" of the prison as he helped gang leaders work out their differences and negotiate prison turf. Without Randall's stamp of approval on me, I don't know what would have happened to me those first years in prison or if I would even be alive today.

Looking back on those days, I realize how naïve I was about prison and the extent of its impact on my life. I had not considered that I would never have homemade pie again or eat with metal utensils from a real plate. I hadn't considered that I would never again touch the rough bark of a tree or feel cool grass under my bare feet. I didn't realize that the last time I petted my dog was the last time I would ever even see a dog. I didn't know then that the last time I made biscuits with my mom would be the last time I would see her smile, hear her laugh, or feel flour on my fingers. Even after that sliver of pie was taken from my tray, I still did not comprehend all the *lasts* that I had experienced as a result of coming to prison. Even today, I occasionally remember something else that I have not tasted, felt, or seen in my twenty years of prison. It's a long list.

I was not a quick study on prison etiquette or survival. My heart would not allow me to accept the dehumanizing way of prison life and simply say "This is the best we can do." All the life and hope had not yet been sucked from my soul. So, in my bright-eyed innocence, I wondered aloud about possibilities for improvement that made most old school convicts laugh out loud. Randall, however, did not laugh. Although he listened intently without expressing an opinion, his actions spoke much louder than words. Right away he took me to see Unit Manager Robertson and told me to tell her about my ideas. At first I was intimidated and afraid that I was being set up for a big joke at my expense. But soon I found myself giving Ms. Robertson the full-court press with positive energy that was not commonly seen in a prison environment.

From that meeting, Ms. Robertson formed an honor unit at the prison. She worked with the warden to identify an existing, drug-infested gang unit so dangerous that prison officers were afraid to work there. The warden decided to break up that unit by sending inmates elsewhere, clearing space to house our new honor pod. Ms. Robertson made Randall and me her clerks, tasked with the job of working together to form a new type of prison community. With 128 beds to fill, we decided to put up posters around the prison:

Honor Pod Residents Wanted

1) Must have a job or go to school

2) Must be disciplinary write-up free for one year

3) Must be non-affiliated with a gang

4) Must be willing to work together to keep the unit clean

The next day we were excited to receive an overwhelming 500 honor pod applications from the 2,000 inmates housed at our prison. Even if it meant more work for us, we didn't want to simply put random inmates in the cells together. So, we began interviewing potential residents and matching up folks for possible cell assignments. Getting two men together to meet and get to know each other a bit seemed a better approach than putting two strangers together to live and share a toilet in only a nine-by-ten–foot space. If they both agreed that they could live together, they would sign a contract agreeing to the basic rules of the pod and to work out any differences in a civil and orderly manner. This contract proved to be a major key to the success of the unit.

Soon all the beds in the honor unit were filled with those selected to begin a new way of prison living—in community. As the men rolled in buggy after buggy of their belongings, they found dirty, nasty cells left behind by those not too thrilled to have been moved out. As new honor unit residents, we decided to have a cleaning party. We brought out our bars of soap, shampoo, and laundry detergent purchased from the commissary and proceeded to scrub every inch of that unit clean. The guard on duty was so astonished that she called Unit Manager Robertson at home to tell her what was going on. Ms. Robertson came to the prison to witness the event and realized just how serious we were about our commitment to living differently and working together in community to accomplish that. She was as excited as we were.

It didn't take long for the honor unit to become *the* place to live among inmates in the entire prison. Qualifying to live in an honor unit gave the men an incentive to get a job and stay out of trouble. The warden recognized the positive impact that it was having and worked to form other types of community living around the prison. Several pods were formed to house men over fifty, and one to house veterans. These units, along with our honor pod, were always part of the tour given to people visiting the prison.

The prison administration noticed that these community-centered pods had no problems with violence, gangs, or finding guards to work there. In fact, most of the guards requested to work in such units. Administrators soon discovered that a surprising number of men at the prison desperately wanted to improve themselves by using honor pod living as a way to prepare for eventual reintegration into society after release from prison. Many who were not in gangs felt that they had been lost in the unavoidable pockets of violence and terror of the other gang-infested units. Not separating those who wish to *do better, live better,* and *be better* from those who wish to continue a path of destruction only allows the negative to prevail. As I learned in my high school math class, a negative multiplied by a positive always equals a negative.

When a member of our honor community made parole or was released, we always had a big party: a *roast*. Those heart-warming, laughter-filled occasions assisted our much-loved brother with his transition back into the Free World. Afterwards, his place in our pod was carefully filled, again using the original process of deliberate and intentional matching and consideration. If Unit Manager Robertson found that a resident failed to maintain a job or school, or could not abide by other provisions of the contract, she quickly moved him to another unit. It was serious business, and it was good.

Ms. Robertson was excited about leading this innovative prison experiment in community living. She found inmate artists and painters to move into the honor unit. They painted beautiful murals on our common space walls. We were proud that our unit looked like an art gallery. We organized walking and exercise clubs, chess clubs, and Biggest Loser contests, collectively losing over a thousand pounds. We cooked together, laughed together, and cried together. I established strong bonds of friendship with men that I still keep in touch with by mail, even though many are now free and doing well in the Free World. One of those men is Randall, who, after nearly thirty years in prison, made parole, is now married, and has a wonderful life on the outside.

During those six years in the honor unit, I still had not learned to heed Randall's advice to embrace and experience the good because it seemed like that good would never end. But even more quickly than it started, my honor pod experience ended as I was transferred without warning from that prison to another one. My friends, my new family, all gone, just like that. My heart was broken, and I felt like it would never recover.

Sadly, this has been my journey during twenty years in seven prisons—and still counting. Each time, I was moved without any notice. Each time, a piece of my heart was ripped away. Eventually, I stopped looking people in the eyes. I fell into the prison posture of looking down, not wanting to make eye contact or develop fellowship with anyone. Losing another friend would have been too hard.

Even if I had had the heart for it, re-creating another honor unit or even developing a sense of community with other inmates again seemed impossible. New Department of Correction officials appeared with a very different model for the prison system. Departmental dictates for stricter, military-style guards and greater regimentation of all prison life left little room for any warden to go off-script. I saw that Tennessee prisons had become like a big industry composed of large warehouses to merely hold human life as it was rotated in and out from one destructive setting to another, apparently without regard for basic human social needs or rehabilitation. When inmates spend years looking down, not making eye contact, not forming bonds of community, and not receiving treatment or skills training, their ability to function declines. As a result, violence and gang activity remained at an all-time high. As a result, inmates usually leave prison much worse than when they came in. As a result, more than half of those getting out of prison will be back.

I became leery of any prison official who spoke of "making things better" because their words were never followed by actions. Most prison employees who strive to make things better are quickly beaten up by a system that doesn't easily tolerate change. In time, these employees become complacent, compliant, or corrupted, or they leave the corrections field altogether. The massive incarceration machine expels those with any vision of positive change.

After years of moving around to different prisons, Randall and I found ourselves at the same prison once again. When I arrived, Randall was about to make parole, and he helped me to get the newspaper editor job that he was leaving. I continued my day-to-day routine of just doing my time, just surviving, without a thought of trying to form community. But, that routine changed the day I met Jeannie, a death-row volunteer who was to become the new prison chaplain, a role that, in the south, is typically held by a white, fundamentalist Christian male. Prison chaplains typically don't embrace anyone who doesn't profess Jesus as Savior, or who is gay. Most inmates were making bets on how long this attractive, sweet, pleasant lady would last among the wolves of inmates and fellow staff members who would surely devour her.

As the newspaper editor, I began to learn more about our new chaplain for a story I was working on. Chaplain Jeannie had been a corporate lawyer in Texas. She also had a degree in religious studies and a history of advocating for the homeless. She had a passion for getting the death sentence abolished and optimistic visions for prison reform. I allowed myself to become hopeful as I learned more about her. I also realized that her enthusiasm for such change would not be easily accepted by prison officials. I even wondered if those in charge of hiring her knew of her positions on criminal justice reform. I was amazed when she looked me in the eyes, truly seeing me and, thereby, forcing me to look up and see her. While in her presence, I felt like the most important person in her world, no rush in conversation, just a real desire that we find each other's humanity. A bright fire of energy had entered the prison, and it would not easily be extinguished.

When Chaplain Jeannie realized that many education rooms were not being used in the evenings, she sought volunteers to come to the prison to teach classes, conduct workshops, and explore possibilities never thought possible behind the razor wire. Soon, over 300 volunteers were on hand to develop programs and work with inmates in a variety of ways that included organizing a pen pal program, pre-release counseling, mentoring, and teaching a range of subjects. In time, a sense of community developed among insiders and outsiders. Inmates who had long ago lost hope of getting out because of a lack of housing or job options found new hope, as volunteers developed friendships with them and opened doors to new relationships, new opportunities, and new possibilities. Supporters started showing up at inmate parole hearings, offering housing and job opportunities that gave the parole board reasons to release well-behaved inmates into the community. Relationships between the inside and outside people fostered informed understanding. This understanding facilitated much-needed legislative recommendations that could only have been prompted by outside people who had benefited from a chance to get to know individual inmates and see them not as generic prisoners, but as real human beings. It is possible.

All faith groups, Christian or not, were given space and time to gather and worship. As we started making eye contact with volunteers, I observed myself and other inmates beginning to look into each other's eyes, really seeing each other's humanity, perhaps for the very first time. A miraculous change came over the prison as the old veil of darkness lifted to let a beam of light shine in—all because of a woman with a passion and a dream that broke through the constraining assumptions of the old system. It is possible.

Through Chaplain Jeannie's mentor program, I met my dear friend Cindy, who transformed my life in the most amazing way. And like me, through this program, hundreds of other inmates also had windows opened to a world they had felt shut out of for so long. The ripple effect of hope spread all around the prison, manifesting in transformed lives and development of a real sense of community and family. It is possible.

Through a contemplative prayer group, I was introduced to Richard, Michael, Bruce, Andrew, Dan, Matt, Valerie, Forrest, and so many others who came to the prison each Saturday night and studied with me and my friends on the inside. We read books on forgiveness, love, and building community, and we always had a passionate discussion on each topic. I realized that many people in the Free World care about those on the inside and want to help them transform their lives. If the system allows it, there is no shortage of kind, loving, and intelligent people who want to walk beyond the "living room" of prison and visit in those areas where inmates really live. Those kind people are open to seeing the suffering and despair found in the hearts of those caged behind bars. Those kind people want to help. It is possible.

Through another program, I found yoga and met the remarkable volunteer instructor, Julie, who, even in her seventies, came each week, dragging the yoga mats along behind her. She gave us valuable lessons, teaching us yoga poses, meditation, and breathing exercises. Even more importantly, she taught us how to live—fully live—in the confines of our limited space and circumstances, recognizing each moment as a special and important moment in our lives. The full meaning of Randall's words was becoming more clear to me as I gained understanding of how unique and amazing each moment of goodness is, especially when those moments are found in a place usually filled with so much despair and destruction. It is possible.

The thought of taking a college class along with Free World students seemed impossible. But professors, such as A. J., Bruce, and others brought their college students to the prison each Monday night so that men in prison blues could learn alongside them, listening to lectures, joining in discussions, writing papers, and reading books brought to us by the professor. We once again felt like part of the outside world as we gained knowledge that no one could take away from us. It is possible.

Then there were Janet, Glenda, and Sam, who organized meaningful workshops and classes promoting inside/out learning. They encouraged us to allow our voices to be heard out in the world through writing, poetry, and art. They gave us avenues that allowed our emotions to emerge, evolve, and find release from the pressure cooker of prison. It is possible.

There was also Michael, who brought us a unique storytelling time when inmates and Free World folk shared insights and reflections about their lives. We learned that everyone's life is filled with many personal stories. We learned that when we begin to understand a person's story, we begin to understand that person as more than just a face in the crowd. That person becomes one in whom you can recognize commonality and a shared humanity. From this comes the empathy and compassion required for a sense of community to develop. It is possible.

The few years I worked with Chaplain Jeannie allowed me to see opportunity in a place where brokenness usually prevails. She was a healing light breaking through our brokenness. Her presence shined so intensely that you couldn't be near it without being enveloped in its warmth. Her vision, thoughts, and ideas, previously so foreign to our system of incarceration, had penetrated the hearts and minds of groups of people, both inside and outside the fence. Her example of unconditional love allowed so many inmates to accept that they were worthy of love, even in the midst of prison. When you are loved, you are able to love others. It is possible.

Chaplain Jeannie's vision was unlike anything I had experienced in all my years in prison. I immediately recognized its goodness and its preciousness. As I participated in making this vision a reality, I recognized that I was also an eyewitness to the history that was being made. I also sadly realized that this candle of infectious light would eventually burn out or be blown out by the system. Just as I feared, it didn't take too long for the drivers of the incarceration machine to notice that the chaplain's work was focusing a spot light on all the cracks in the system. As a result, prison administrators began making it increasingly difficult for outsiders to enter the prison and conduct their programs and services. Knowing her work was far from over, Chaplain Jeannie eventually made the agonizing choice to leave the place in which she had been called to minister in order to more aggressively advocate for prison reform. She gathered volunteers and formed an organization in the Free World to tackle some of the urgently needed changes to the prison system. So her love continues in new ways today. It is possible.

I and many of the other men who experienced the revelation of change with Chaplain Jeannie have been dispersed around the state to various prisons. We took with us the knowledge that building a community of love and support can happen wherever we are, even in prison. It is possible.

I have no regrets about allowing myself to lift my eyes and look up with hope. I refuse to lower my gaze and drop out of life again. I need to speak out, and I have through many essays about little-known aspects of prison life. I need to truly see others. I need to hear their stories of life, death, and suffering. I need to share the humanity we all have in common. Randall's words have finally reached my heart, now making perfect sense. I'll grab every possible moment of good and experience each one of them fully, in that moment. It is possible.

Change: It Is Possible

How do you know if a seed will bear food
    and feed a community?
You don't, you just plant it.

How do you know if there will be water
    in the ground where you dig to quench the thirst of men?
You don't, you just dig.

How do you know if your letter
    will convey your request for help?
You don't, you just write.

How do you know if the homeless woman will
    use your donated money wisely?
You don't, you just give.

How do you know if your presence will
    make any difference?
You don't, you just show up.

How do you know if your love will be
    returned or forgotten or misused?
You don't, you just love.

It is possible to change the world
But it must start with you.

It's Been Too Long

I've lost the sound of your tender melodic voice

amongst the screaming of foul-tongued men spewing profanity.

I've lost the touch of your hand and your delicate fingers

amongst the feel of steel and shackles cutting at my skin.

I've lost the rose-petaled smell of your silky skin

amongst the stench of sweat and shit.

I've lost the softness and wisdom of your eyes

amongst the cold gray stares from strangers and oppressors.

My sensations numbed

from deliberate removal from life—real life.

I've been banded like a homing pigeon

bound to its owner—

always marked:

"If found return to . . ."

How long is too long?

How long before I don't want to remember,

can't remember?

I'M HERE

WHERE ARE YOU?

DON'T FORGET ME

About the Author

Tony D. Vick

Tony Vick was born in 1962, in Clarksville, Tennessee, into a home of Southern Baptist parents and an older brother. His father was a barber and gospel singer, and his mother was a stay-at-home mom. Tony's parents and brother have all died during Tony's incarceration. After excelling in high school, Tony received the "Outstanding Business Student" award and a scholarship to study business at the University of Tennessee. He worked in retail sales, banking, and, at one time, owned and operated a Southern-style restaurant.

Tony entered prison twenty years ago after living thirty-four years in Freedomsville as a closeted gay man. He is currently serving two life sentences for murder. While in prison, Tony has worked as a GED teaching assistant, clerk, and prison newspaper editor. He has been involved with Inside-Out prison programs where Free World college students travel to prisons and join incarcerated students as classmates in post-secondary courses built around dialogue, collaboration, and experiential learning. Between 2010 and 2014, Tony completed five semesters in Vanderbilt University's Divinity School Inside-Out program.

In 2013, Tony's essay, "Look at Me," was published in a book, *Turning Teaching Inside Out: A Pedagogy of Transformation for Community-Based Education,* by Simone Weil Davis and Barbara Sherr Roswell. In 2015, Tony's story and thoughts on forgiveness were included in Michael T. McRay's book *Where the River Bends: Considering Forgiveness in the Lives of Prisoners.* Tony continues to write essays and poetry that challenge readers to address prison reform as one of the most important social issues of this generation.

Tony can be reached via Cindy Ford at:

cindy@johnfordconsulting.com

About the Author

Michael T. McRay

Michael T. McRay is a writer, advocate, educator, and speaker, living in Nashville, Tennessee. He is the author of *Where the River Bends: Considering Forgiveness in the Lives of Prisoners* (Cascade, 2015), with a foreword by Desmond M. Tutu, and *Letters from "Apartheid Street": A Christian Peacemaker in Occupied Palestine* (Cascade, 2013). As an adjunct instructor at Lipscomb University in Nashville, Michael has taught courses inside Riverbend Maximum Security Institution and the Tennessee

Prison for Women as part of Lipscomb's LIFE program. In Fall 2015, hired as a Visiting Scholar at Texas Christian University, Michael spent two months traveling through Israel-Palestine, Northern Ireland, and South Africa conducting over fifty interviews about the complexities of pursuing reconciliation in divided societies. He is currently crafting a new book on this experience.

He is the cofounder of No Exceptions Prison Collective (noexceptions.net) and founded, organizes, and co-hosts Tenx9 Nashville (www.tenx9nashville.com), a Belfast-originated monthly community storytelling night for the sharing of true life stories around a theme. Michael also facilitates story exchanges as a Master Practitioner with Narrative 4. He volunteered at Riverbend Prison for over four years and served as a volunteer prison chaplain for nearly one year before being banned by the warden in April 2014 for organizing on behalf of the inmates.

Michael holds an MPhil (with *Distinction*) in Conflict Resolution and Reconciliation Studies from Trinity College Dublin at Belfast, as well as a BA in History from Lipscomb University. He speaks often, and his work has been published, discussed, and reviewed on websites and in print publications like *Plough Magazine, The Porch Magazine, Leaven Journal, Englewood Review of Books, Experimental Theology, The Tokens Show Blog, Middle East Experience, The Examiner*, and *Red Letter Christians*.

Get in touch at:

www.michaelmcray.com

Bibliography

ACLU. *At America's Expense: The Mass Incarceration of the Elderly.* New York: American Civil Liberties Union, 2012.

Bonhoeffer, Dietrich. *Letters and Papers from Prison.* New York: Touchstone, 2007.

Chiu, Tina. *It's About Time: Aging Prisoners, Increasing Costs, and Geriatic Release.* Center on Sentencing and Corrections, New York: Vera Institute of Justice, 2010.

Frankl, Victor. *Man's Search for Meaning.* Boston: Beacon, 2006.

Gottschalk, Marie. *Caught: The Prison State and the Lockdown of American Politics.* Princeton, NJ: Princeton University Press, 2015.

Moyne, John, and Catherine Barks. *Open Secret: Versions of Rumi.* Boulder, CO: Shambhala, 1999.

Nouwen, Henri. *Reaching Out: The Three Movements of the Spiritual Life.* New York: Doubleday, 1975.

Ó Tuama, Pádraig. *Sorry for Your Troubles.* Norwich: Canterbury, 2013.

Ogletree, Charles, and Austin Sarat, eds. *Life Without Parole: America's New Death Penalty?* New York: NYU Press, 2012.

Orwell, George. *The Collected Essays, Journalism and Letters of George Orwell, Volume 4 1945–1950.* Edited by Sonia Orwell, & Ian Angus. Wilmington, MA: Mariner, 1971.

Schreiber, Jon. *Child of Existence, Child of Society.* Oakland, CA: The Breema Center, 2015.

Printed in Great Britain
by Amazon

86471870R00073